ENDANGERED SPECIES OF THE WORLD

ENDANGERED SPECIES OF THE WORLD

Laura O' Biso Socha

Friedman Group

A FRIEDMAN GROUP BOOK

Copyright © 1991 by Michael Friedman Publishing Group, Inc.

ISBN 0-7924-5305-2

ENDANGERED SPECIES OF THE WORLD
was prepared and produced by
Michael Friedman Publishing Group, Inc.
15 West 26th Street
New York, New York 10010

Editor: Sharyn Rosart
Art Director: Jeff Batzli
Designer: Robert W. Kosturko
Photography Researcher: Daniella Jo Nilva

Typeset by Bookworks Plus
Color separation by Excel Graphic Arts Co.
Printed and bound in Hong Kong by Leefung-Asco Printers, Ltd.

For Maia: Wolf, Teacher, Companion, Friend

It would be impossible to list the names of everyone who assisted in the research and writing of this book, and so I offer my sincere appreciation and thanks to all of you.
My special thanks to the organizations and individuals who gave so freely of their time and offered their support for this project. Special thanks to Defenders of Wildlife, Rainforest Action Network, Greenpeace, and Earth First! Wolf Action Network.

Contents

INTRODUCTION:
A HOLE IN THE WORLD

The last word in ignorance is the man who says of an
animal or plant: "What good is it?"

—Aldo Leopold

What good is it? That uniquely human attitude toward other life-forms on this planet has contributed to more deaths—animal, plant, insect, and human—than one can comprehend. From the time the earth was very young, nature has held all Earth's elements in a delicate, complex balance. Each living thing, every plant and flower, every animal, every rock and drop of water, has its place and purpose. Nature lived and flourished long before the first human stood upright and began to think.

To native people around the world, and especially to Native Americans, the concept of natural balance was easily understood. Mother Earth and Father Sky—gifts to the human race from the Creator—would provide humans with everything they needed. All they had to do in return was give thanks and use the gifts of the Creator wisely.

Native people recognized that everything in nature was connected and related to everything else, even though humans might not easily be able to see how or why. They realized that because of this interdependency, humans were part of life on Earth, not superior to it. They knew something that modern man has forgotten: the earth, nature itself, can live long, well, and probably better,

Left: King Kong at home. The gentle mountain gorillas have shown mankind that they are not like the monsters that Hollywood has created. Virtually unknown to the western hemisphere prior to 1869, the giant panda (previous page) is now one of the world's most beloved, and endangered, species.

without the human race—but the human race could not survive to the end of this sentence without nature.

For all of its collective intelligence, the human race has been painfully slow in realizing that simple fact. A frightening number of individuals of this species still do not understand it. These are the individuals who are apt to ask, "What good is it?"

The "good" of an animal cannot be explained easily, especially if explanation is attempted strictly from a technical standpoint. Why should we care that some slimy frog in a jungle halfway around the world is dying? Who cares if we never see another wolf—most of us have never seen one anyway. People in New York aren't going to die because somebody in Africa cut off the head of another gorilla. What difference does it make that animals we don't even know exist are dying along with the rain forests?

Let's look at these questions another way: Picture the earth as a tapestry, finely woven in a myriad of patterns, colors, and textures that make up the planet. Every living thing is woven into this work of art, from the tiniest microbe in the sea to the elephants in Africa, from one pole to another, from east to west and back again at the equator.

The threads that are the people of the world are intertwined with the threads of other life-forms. Each and every thread depends on the position and strength of the others to keep it in place, in balace, with the overall picture presented in the tapestry. All of the threads are touching and being touched by each other to form one glorious pattern.

Now take a scissors and cut one thread in this priceless tapestry. Cut anywhere—it doesn't

The howl of the timber wolf was once heard throughout North America, but the animals had already been systematically exterminated from nearly all of their former range by the mid 1800s.

matter where the hole begins, and cut only one thread—one is all that is necessary. Now pull that severed thread, and watch as the tiny hole becomes larger. As you pull, consider how the threads let go of each other and come apart. Watch as the form, color, texture, and beauty of that priceless tapestry unravel before your eyes, and fall away to nothingness. Where are you in the pattern?

Our planet is presently suffering from innumerable holes. There is a hole in the sky, in the protective ozone of our atmosphere. There are black holes of dead, polluted nothingness in the oceans. And there are holes in the pattern of life, where thousands of animal, plant, and some human species have perished.

Yet there are some bright spots scattered among the dark holes of the future. The first threads of comprehension are beginning to penetrate the human mind: people are beginning to realize that we are destroying our home, our fellow species, and in the process, ourselves. Public concern is shifting from the threat of nuclear war to concern about environmental threats that are much more realistic—and infinitely more serious.

Admittedly, it has taken us an embarrassingly long time to reach this understanding. Henry David Thoreau wrote in 1860, "What is the use of a house if you haven't got a tolerable planet to put it on?" More than 130 years later, we are still asking the same question. The difference is that now we're finally paying attention to the answer.

One nice thing about a tapestry: if you gather up all the loose threads in time, it can be repaired. People around the world are grasping the loose threads of the earth, tying knots, finding ways to stop, and maybe reverse, the unraveling. Grab a thread. It's not too late.

LIVING ON THE EDGE

Endangered species are living on the edge of extinction. The distance between extinction and survival is a narrow corridor in time, a buffer zone between life and death that shifts with the whims of humankind. It is, at best, a precarious place to be.

For some, this ever-changing buffer zone squeezes a bit too hard, and the space becomes too small. The species dies. For others, being "endangered," has given them another chance to cling to the edge of survival. The difference lies in making "The List."

DEFINING ENDANGERMENT

The American Endangered Species Act (ESA) of 1973 established an official process for recognizing American and foreign species that were in danger of extinction. The act outlined procedures for determining a species's status and for listing the species as endangered or "threatened." It also provided outlines for establishing recovery plans so that the species could eventually be "delisted."

The ESA has been called the most important wildlife legislation in the world, for it imposes severe restrictions on U.S. trade, import, and possession of endangered animals, their parts, and/or products made from them, effectively impacting the market around the world.

The ESA provided full protection to species determined to be endangered, and also provided government funding for implementation of the process. That's where it ran into trouble. Long-term authority for providing government funds expired in 1985, but budget cuts went into effect as early as 1981, when the Reagan administration deleted funding for the Land and Water Conservation Fund. Acquisition of refuge land to protect wildlife habitats is most critical to species survival. It does not benefit a species to recover their populations if they have no place to go.

The ESA has been amended many times since 1973, but substantial improvements that strengthened the ESA were not signed into law until October 1988. Under those amendments, government agencies administering endangered and threatened species must also monitor candidate species, list species in immediate danger, monitor populations of recovered species, standardize recovery plans, increase penalties for violators, include damage to listed plants as violations, increase support to landowners wishing to provide for endangered species on their land, and increase funding.

Though far from perfect, the Endangered Species Act does improve the survival chances of species that earn the dubious distinction of "making the list." And, despite the political problems that surround any government-sponsored effort, the ESA has set a conservation effort example that continues to have worldwide impact.

Beginning in 1975 with the signatures of just ten world governments, the Convention on International Trade in Endangered Species (CITES) has grown to be the most widely supported and strongest of many international efforts for species conservation. Nearly 100 nations have signed the

Black rhinos, which once roamed freely in Africa, are now not totally safe from poachers even within a fenced rhino preserve.

CITES treaty, which not only regulates trade in endangered species, but also requires governments to monitor the environmental status of species within their jurisdiction.

CITES made history in October 1989, when delegates from seventy-six nations voted to place the elephant on the CITES endangered species list, thus imposing a worldwide ban on the sale or purchase of ivory. In ten years' time, 1.3 million African elephants have been slaughtered for their ivory. An estimated 625,000 survive today.

Thousands of independent environmental conservation groups have organized around the world in the last twenty years. Through their memberships, the people voice their support for stronger actions against violators, the importance of land and water conservation, public education, and conservation legislation.

Through these combined efforts, a very few species have recovered sufficiently to be "delisted," but the statistics are far too low to brag about. In one year's time, according to U.S. Fish and Wildlife Service records (for U.S. species only), one species, the Palau dove, was delisted due to recovery. Six species perished.

There are 1,072 endangered and threatened species listed worldwide as of March 1990. This figure includes plants, which are usually excluded when the average person thinks about endangered species. However, plants are a chief ingredient of habitat, and without habitat, there can be no wildlife.

The remains of an African elephant (above) bear silent testimony to the slaughter. A family of African elephants (right) displays the tusks that often cost them their lives.

Thousands of species that may be in danger of extinction have not been listed simply because we don't know enough about them—or possibly anything about them. For instance, it has been estimated that just 2.5 acres (1 ha) of tropical rain forest may be home to 42,000 different species of insects, and that four square miles (10 km²) of rain forest may harbor 1,500 different plants, 125 mammal species, nearly 800 different trees, 400 different birds, and at least 100 different reptiles. Some of these may be species we haven't yet discovered.

Preservation of endangered habitats is a critical part of every species recovery plan. Many species require specific habitats, and are not capable of adapting to another environment.

Certain species also require movement and must have adequate territory to fulfill their needs. Defenders of Wildlife has initiated a campaign to link major habitat fragments by means of dedicated "corridors," which will allow wildlife to wander through their habitats and will reduce the number of roadkills.

PRESERVING HABITATS, PRESERVING LIFE

When we think of endangered species, we tend to think only in terms of wildlife—but not all endangered species have fur, wings, scales, or skin. Some have plants, water, rocks, trees. They have different names: rain forest, desert, ocean, wetland, marsh, swamp, field, river, tundra, mountain, ravine, roadside.

Left: A pleasure boat slices through the home territory of the Florida manatee, ignoring posted warnings. Above: A diver attempts to attach a radio tag to a Florida manatee to help biologists monitor its movements and habits.

They are as diverse in form, function, and number as the species that depend on them for survival. They are living entities that change, evolve, and have withstood eons of earth time—yet humanity is capable of completely obliterating them in the course of a day. They are the environment, the habitats, the vital organs of Earth. We tend to look at these habitats as being less important than the animals that live in them, yet these creatures depend on the health and availability of their environment for survival. We tend to forget that we, the human race, who possess the godlike power to obliterate the environment, are in the process, obliterating the chances for our own survival.

As you read about the endangered species of the world in this book and in others, you will see again and again as a major cause of a species' decline the phrase *habitat destruction*.

To survive, a grizzly bear needs the ecological niche that produced it: a vast, unspoiled range, free of human encroachment. A three-toed sloth spends its entire life in the treetops of tropical rain forests, to which it is perfectly adapted. Likewise, the vaquita, a small porpoise discovered in 1958, exists only in the Gulf of California. Island habitats—Hawaii, Australia, New Zealand, the Galapagos—are home to species that are found nowhere else in the world.

Unless suitable habitats are preserved, it makes little sense to preserve vanishing species. In many cases, it is impossible. Animals that exist only in zoo cages have lost contact with the condi-

Above: Safe, but not free: Life in a zoo cage can't compare with this snow leopard's native mountains of Nepal. Right: Ocean waters are home to a group of sea otters, and a toxic dumping ground for mankind.

tions that give meaning to their existence, and are a poor, often unhealthy, substitute for creatures living naturally in the wild.

Unfortunately, for some, habitat loss has become so great a problem that for now, zoos and holding areas are the only places these animals can currently survive.

The shrinking habitats of animals such as the giant panda and Asian elephant, for example, have already taken their toll. Once able to move to new feeding grounds, pandas surrounded by human development instead starved to death during a die-off of bamboo, their life source.

It is also likely that when the waters of the Gulf of California become toxic enough to kill, the vaquitas will die off and become extinct (if people don't kill them first), for that, as far as we know, is their only habitat on earth.

Again and again this tragic turn of events is repeated, for each and every endangered or threatened species on the planet. Among the most disturbing situations, however, are those where the potential to set aside a secured habitat exists but has been denied. The old cliché, "all dressed up and no place to go," might be applied to species on recovery program/release site "waiting lists." For many of them, time is critical. Red tape, procedure, and protocol often hurt them rather than help their predicament.

For example, Mexican wolves being held in captivity are actually evolving into domesticated animals that may not survive on their own when officials and governments finally agree on a suitable release area. The shame is greater when suitable sites exist but are politically influenced, controlled, and denied.

On the brighter side are the changes in attitudes that people around the world are beginning to express concerning the cleanup and preservation of the environment and in turn, in the preservation of not only endangered species, but of all species.

In some circles, what has been called "global rethinking" is replacing "military thinking." According to Worldwatch Institute, for example, the $12 million it would cost for one nuclear weapons test could instead be used to install 80,000 hand pumps in Third World villages, providing access to safe drinking water.

Some other statistics and suggestions to consider: a 10-foot (3-m) pile of newspapers recycled saves at least one tree. A 1.7 mile (3 km) per gallon increased efficiency in motor vehicles would conserve more oil than is estimated to be within the Arctic National Wildlife Refuge. If 100 million trees could be planted by 1992, carbon dioxide emissions would be reduced by 18 million tons (16 million t) per year. And by the year 2000, if present rates of growth continue, the world population is expected to reach 6 billion.

Working together, that many individuals of a superior species should at least manage to preserve the earth. Working together toward that goal must begin now, with the actions of each individual. It is possible to restore the natural balance of the earth. Humans must alter their way of thinking, change the way that they view fellow species and the environment, the land, the earth. This planet is our home, our life. It is called Mother Earth for a reason.

ENDANGERED MAMMALS

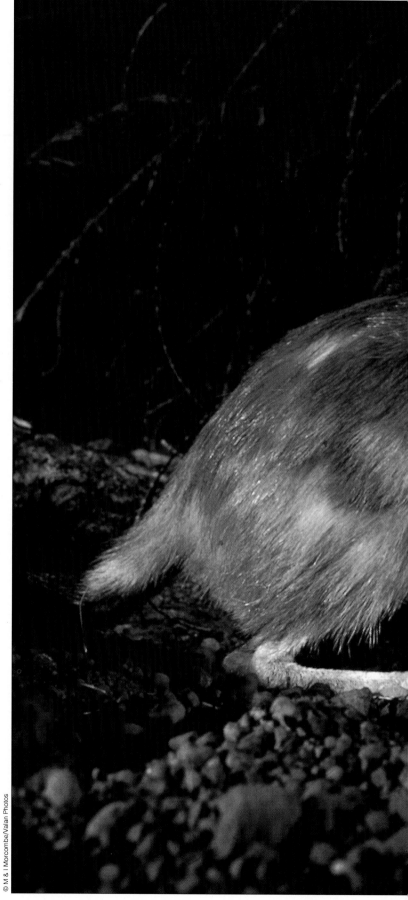

RABBIT BANDICOOT

Bandicoots are a group of nocturnal, ratlike marsupials native to Australia and New Guinea. They are noted for their peculiar gait, a combination of jumping and running. There are about twenty-two species of bandicoot.

Unlike other marsupials (which are generally defined as mammals that do not develop placenta, and have an abdominal pouch for carrying young), bandicoots have a placenta. Two to six young are born after a gestation period of only twelve to fifteen days, and spend about two months in the mother's pouch.

Several members of the bandicoot family are on the Endangered Species List. Perhaps the rarest is the rabbit bandicoot *(Macrotis lagotis)*, the only surviving species of this particular family; the lesser bandicoot *(Macrotis leucura)* is now extinct.

Rabbit bandicoots, called "bilbies" in Australia, are named for their rabbitlike ears. Small, isolated populations survive only in the arid interior regions.

Bilbies are solitary animals that live in burrows that may extend six or seven feet (2 m) underground. The burrow shelters the bandicoot from the day's heat. The animal forages for insects, beetles, and termites during the cooler nighttime hours.

A cousin of the rabbit bandicoot, the pig-footed bandicoot *(Chaeropus ecaudatus)*, is so named for the two heavily nailed toes on its forefeet and one heavily nailed toe on its hind feet that give the appearance of hooves. This animal may now be extinct—the last confirmed sighting in the wild was in the 1920s.

Bandicoots are considered pests by farmers and ranchers and have been routinely exterminated. Those on the endangered list are not protected.

RABBIT BANDICOOT

Macrotis lagotis

Historical Range: Central and northwestern Australia.

Current Range: Australian interior.

Estimated Wild Population: Unknown.

Estimated Captive Population: Unknown, but as of 1986 four rabbit bandicoots were living in zoos.

Major Threats: Routinely exterminated by farmers and ranchers who consider them pests.

Conservation Efforts: Protected as endangered species.

Young barred bandicoots (far left) and a mature rabbit bandicoot (left) are two unusual and rare species of Australian marsupials.

© Ken Cole

BROWN OR GRIZZLY BEAR

"Lions . . . and tigers . . . and bears, Oh my!" Those familiar lines from *The Wizard of Oz* may creep into the mind of anyone who ventures alone into the woods of North America, but it's not the lions and tigers that really inspire worry. Anybody can handle a lion or tiger—they're just overgrown cats—but bears are another story!

Bears are distantly related to dogs, wolves, coyotes, and foxes, having evolved from a common ancestor some 40 million years ago. Like their canid "relatives," bears are carnivores, possessing large canine teeth, plus molars for grinding the vegetation that makes up much of their diet.

One of the largest bears in North America is the brown bear, which may or may not be brown. The fur actually ranges in color from cinnamon to reddish blond to brown to black. Brown bears are distinguished from other bears not by color, then, but by the hump at their shoulders. Often, silver-tipped guard hairs give the animal a grizzled appearance—hence the name grizzly.

An adult grizzly averages about four feet (1.2 m) at the shoulder and weighs about 500 pounds (225 kg), though record weights of more than 1,000 pounds (450 kg) have been recorded. In spite of its ponderous appearance, a grizzly can manage to move at speeds of up to 25 miles (40 km) an hour, and they have been known to kill moose, deer, and horses with one swipe of the paw.

Brown bears once roamed over most of the states west of the Mississippi River and into Mexico, but were shot on sight if the opportunity presented itself. Destruction of the grizzly began with the

BROWN BEAR
Ursus arctos horribilis

Historical Range: Holarctic (continuous around the world north of the tropics, excluding ocean barriers). In the U.S.A., brown bears once roamed most states west of the Mississippi. Their range extended south to Mexico and north to Canada and Alaska.

Current Range: Alaska, Canada, British Columbia; smaller populations in Montana, Wyoming, Idaho.

Estimated Wild Population: Approximately 2,500 to 3,000 in Alaska's Kodiak National Wildlife Refuge; less than 900 in lower forty-eight states. Wild population estimates for Mexico are not available, but it is listed as a Mexican endangered species.

Estimated Captive Population: Some brown bears live in zoos and circuses; the actual number is unavailable.

Major threats: Habitat loss from mining and logging operations; campers, hikers, and developers encroach on their territory; hunting and poaching for skin, head trophies, and claws further endanger their numbers.

Conservation Efforts: Listed as a threatened species on the U.S. list. Public education about human/bear encounters. Efforts to ensure adequate habitat protection, including maintaining restricted areas off limits to humans. Increased penalties for poachers and stricter law enforcement.

When given the choice, brown bears, or grizzlies, prefer to avoid contact with humans, but increased recreational use of wilderness areas has resulted in more frequent encounters between bears and humans. The brown bear commands the most respect; an adult bear can kill a moose with one swipe of its paw and can move with surprising speed and agility.

Lewis and Clark expedition and continued unchecked through the 1930s. It slowed then only because there were no more brown bears left in California, Oregon, and the Southwest.

In the lower forty-eight states, brown bears remain in Yellowstone National Park, Glacier National Park, parts of Idaho and northwestern Washington, and portions of Montana. In Alaska, they are called Alaskan brown bears, and while the populations there are stable, they are far short of their former numbers.

The brown bear is classified as threatened on the U.S. Endangered and Threatened Species List, with the exception of the brown bears found in Mexico. These are listed as endangered.

Encounters with humans must be minimized in order for the grizzly to survive. The bear requires a considerable area of wilderness in which to roam, and existing habitats are shrinking as humans spend more time logging, mining, camping, hiking, and hunting in grizzly territory.

A grizzly bear (above) poses on top of a rushing waterfall. Grizzlies are normally solitary animals, but tolerate each other when they gather in numbers for the seasonal run of salmon. An Alaskan brown bear sow is followed by her three cubs (right). The future of these animals is uncertain, for brown bears are not yet fully protected and are sometimes poached for their hides, head trophies, and claws.

© Leonard Rue Enterprises/FPG International

BACTRIAN CAMEL

More commonly known in the Western world as the "two-humped" camel, the bactrian has long been domesticated as a pack animal in its native China and Mongolia, but the natural, wild populations that live in the Gobi Desert are very close to extinction.

The bactrian differs from its more popular one-humped cousin, the dromedary, in its possession of a coat of long, shaggy hair, which is shed during the summer months.

Camels are uniquely adapted to their environment. The humps of the camel reserve fat and provide nourishment to the animal in times when food is difficult to obtain—not an uncommon situation in the harsh desert habitat. It was once thought that the hump stored water—but that

This juvenile bactrian camel (opposite page) will never see its native land, the sands of the Gobi Desert. Bactrian camels have long been domesticated and are easily bred as zoo animals. Above: Truly wild populations of pure bactrians are the endangered species. One-humped hybrids are crosses between bactrian and dromedary camels. Feral camels also breed with wild bactrians.

BACTRIAN CAMEL
Camelus bactrianus

———

Historic Range: Mongolia and China.

Current Range: Scattered populations in former ranges.

Estimated Wild Population: Less than 1,000.

Estimated Captive Population: In zoos, circuses, and private ownerships.

Major Threats: Loss of habitats due to growing human population; pure wild populations threatened by feral camels (domestic animals that have been released).

Conservation Efforts: Habitat preservation. Preservation of truly wild gene pools.

© Greg Vaughn/Tom Stack & Associates

The long, winter coat of this bactrian camel (above) protects it from the harsh weather conditions of its native Mongolia and China. Once shed, the camel's wool is made into clothing and blankets. It was once thought that the humps on the camel's back stored water, but we now know that the humps reserve fat and supply nutrients when food is scarce.

function is actually accomplished by the lining of the camel's stomach. Thirsty camels have been known to drink up to twenty-seven gallons (102 l) of water during one drinking session!

Other unique adaptations enable the camel to survive well in the desert. A specialized eyelid wipes sand particles from the surface of the eye. Nostrils close off to become mere slits, keeping flying sand out of the camel's nose. The camel's feet—with two thick toes to a foot, each with a broad, flat pad—are highly adapted to walking on shifting sands. The bones grow sideways to give added support.

The dromedary is preferred as a pack and riding animal and has been domesticated to a greater extent than the bactrian. Hybrids, single-humped crosses between dromedaries and bactrian camels, are favored because of their strength and endurance. Thus, breeding of pure bactrians has been practiced only in Central Asia, where the climate is too severe even for hybrids.

Bactrians are relatively numerous as zoo animals, but their wild populations are not so fortunate, numbering less than 1,000 animals.

© Kennon Cooke/Valan Photos

The tusks of the African elephant (above) are really modified incisors which serve the elephant in a variety of ways. An elephant's voracious appetite keeps it constantly feeding (above right). Elephants routinely transform heavily forested jungles into open grasslands, creating habitats for other species.

ELEPHANT

Can you imagine India and Africa without elephants? The thought seems farfetched and certainly unacceptable to anyone with any affinity for wildlife. But an elephantless India is very near to becoming a reality, and an Africa without elephants follows uncomfortably close behind.

These two species of elephant, the largest land mammal in the world, are the living remains of a once widely distributed group of huge, herbivorous animals that inhabited most of the earth.

According to *Buffon's System of Natural History,* published in 1811, "the elephants are more numerous in Africa than in Asia," an observation that remains true today. The African elephant, *Loxodonta africana,* is listed as a threatened species, while its counterpart, the Asian elephant, *Elephas maximus,* has been given endangered status. The Asian elephant has suffered mostly from loss of habitat from the human population explosion. Both species have succumbed to widespread, ruthless hunting and poaching for their tusks, the major threat today for the elephants of Africa.

Elephants themselves have been sometimes blamed for habitat destruction. It doesn't take very long for a group of elephants to transform a heavily forested jungle into an open plain. But the elephants' voracious appetites are beneficial in the long run, creating open grasslands that support a multitude of grazing species, which in turn provide sustenance for the predators. The elephant in this way helps to keep nature in balance.

Both species of elephant grow marvelous tusks, which are actually modified incisors. When detached from an elephant (which must be dead in order for this gruesome task to be accomplished) the tusk becomes ivory and is valued with gold, silver, gemstones, and jewels. People who look at a

© Gerry Ellis/Ellis Wildlife Collection

fine piece of ivory jewelry or who admire an ivory carving forget (or are completely unaware) that it cost an elephant its life.

Over 90 percent of the ivory being circulated in the world today comes from elephants killed illegally. To meet the demand for roughly 800 tons (720 t) of ivory per year, an estimated 90,000 or more elephants die. Enough mother elephants are included in this figure to increase the numbers of dead by about 10,000—these are the orphaned young, which die of starvation.

The elephant is the largest living land mammal. A male African elephant stands eleven to twelve feet (3-4 m) at the shoulder, and weighs upwards of 12,000 pounds (5,400 kg). An elephant calf nurses from its mother until it is four or five years old—usually when the next calf is born. Elephants reach sexual maturity at about twelve years of age, but males are not really sexually active until they are in their thirties. Unless their lives are prematurely ended, elephants live for well over fifty years.

Elephant herds exhibit some remarkable displays of concern for each other. Injured elephants are fed and encouraged by others, and dead elephants young and old have been buried by survivors. Following page: Millions of elephants once roamed freely throughout the African continent. Poaching for ivory has reduced their numbers to about 625,000.

AFRICAN ELEPHANT
Loxodonta africana

Historical Range: Millions of elephants once roamed throughout the African continent.

Current Range: Presently extinct in North Africa; scattered groups remain in sub-Saharan Africa.

Estimated Wild Population: Approximately 625,000 (less than half of what it was ten years ago).

Estimated Captive Population: Fairly common in zoos and circuses.

Major Threats: Poaching for ivory.

Conservation Efforts: A CITES treaty bans trade in ivory internationally, but a number of countries refuse to comply. Currently officially listed as a threatened species on the ESA, which provides only a temporary ban on ivory trade in the United States. Conservation efforts under way for "endangered" listing and to encourage boycott of ivory products.

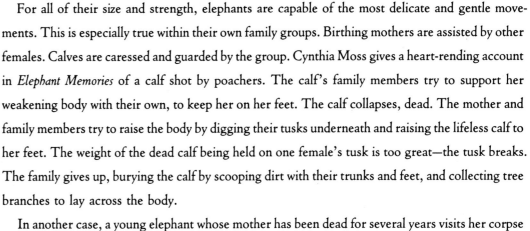

For all of their size and strength, elephants are capable of the most delicate and gentle movements. This is especially true within their own family groups. Birthing mothers are assisted by other females. Calves are caressed and guarded by the group. Cynthia Moss gives a heart-rending account in *Elephant Memories* of a calf shot by poachers. The calf's family members try to support her weakening body with their own, to keep her on her feet. The calf collapses, dead. The mother and family members try to raise the body by digging their tusks underneath and raising the lifeless calf to her feet. The weight of the dead calf being held on one female's tusk is too great—the tusk breaks. The family gives up, burying the calf by scooping dirt with their trunks and feet, and collecting tree branches to lay across the body.

In another case, a young elephant whose mother has been dead for several years visits her corpse frequently, gently touching and moving the skull.

Perhaps humans can learn some tenderness from the elephant, instead of slaughtering it for meaningless trinkets.

A recent ban on the ivory trade may help to curtail some of the poaching that takes place, but some countries have already declared they will not honor the restrictions. Shrinking habitats, as well as poaching for their ivory tusks, have greatly reduced the number of Asian elephants. Approximately 40,000 of these animals survive in portions of Southeast Asia, including India, Sri Lanka, and Sumatra.

ASIAN ELEPHANT

Elephas maximus

Historical Range: All of south central and Southeast Asia.

Current Range: Southeast Asia, India, Sri Lanka, Sumatra.

Estimated Wild Population: Approximately 40,000.

Estimated Captive Population: In zoos and on reserves.

Major Threats: Habitat destruction due to expanding human population, widespread poaching for ivory.

Conservation Efforts: CITES treaty banned international ivory trade in October 1989, but several countries—including China, Great Britain, South Africa, Botswana, Zambia, and Zimbabwe—have submitted reservations to the ban, meaning they would resume CITES-controlled trade. Habitat destruction continues due to booming human population. More emphasis and media coverage is presently focused on the African elephant.

Loss of habitat is the major reason for the decline in the number of Indian elephants (below). Exploding human populations encroach on available space. The largest numbers of Indian elephants today are domesticated animals. Right: Domesticated Indian elephants refresh themselves in the Manas River in Assam, India. Domestication and the continually shrinking habitat available for wild elephants are factors that will affect the future of this species.

BLACK-FOOTED FERRET
Mustela nigripes

Historic Range: The Dakotas and Montana south to northern Texas, New Mexico, and parts of Arizona. Western Canada.

Current Range: One small colony discovered in Wyoming; present population below viable breeding levels.

Estimated Wild Population: Unknown.

Estimated Captive Population: Less than 100.

Major Threats: Poisoning, predation, distemper and other diseases; loss of suitable habitat and prey species.

Conservation Efforts: Captive breeding/recovery program administered by ESA is trying to bring the population up to viable levels and is looking for suitable release sites. Search continues for existing wild populations. Advocates trying to ban poisons used in predator-control programs.

The black-footed ferret is thought to be one of the most endangered mammals in the United States. The ferret population was inadvertently decimated when livestock ranchers set out to exterminate the prairie dogs by using strychnine and other nonselective poisons.

© Stephen J. Krasemann/Valan Photos

BLACK-FOOTED FERRET

The black-footed ferret has been called the most endangered mammal in North America. In the early 1980s, wildlife biologists were ready to write the ferret off as an extinct species when a few of these elusive critters were discovered in a prairie dog village in Wyoming.

Ironically, it was the prairie dogs, not the ferrets, that were targeted for destruction. Toward the end of the 1800s, it was estimated that some 5 billion prairie dogs inhabited North America. Livestock ranchers waged war on the rodents (which were accused of eating vegetation meant for cattle and sheep) with strychnine and other nonselective poisons.

The black-footed ferret preyed heavily on prairie dogs, and used prairie dog tunnels as their own dens. In the process of killing off the prairie dogs, the ferret population was decimated, and until the discovery in 1981, they were thought to be extinct.

The black-footed ferret is the wild relative of the domesticated ferrets that are popular household pets. They are members of the weasel family and are distinguished from their relatives by the dark raccoonlike mask on the face, black-tipped tail, and of course, black feet.

The black-footed ferret may be one endangered species on the road to recovery. Since the discovery in Wyoming, scientists have monitored this small colony to learn what they could about ferret ecology. By 1984, they estimated the wild population to be around 129 animals.

Disaster struck the ferrets again in 1985, however, when a distemper epidemic swept through the colony. Surviving ferrets were captured and placed in a captive breeding program, which has proven to be successful in terms of producing healthy animals. Finding suitable release sites with a substantial prey base to relocate the ferrets may be the most difficult task ahead.

© Gerry Ellis/Ellis Wildlife Collection

Pandora (left), a mountain gorilla in Rwanda. Dian Fossey pioneered the study of these animals and was killed in Rwanda for her efforts. Below: The western world's impression of the gorilla has always been one of a savage killer, a monster. Gorillas are, in fact, peaceful vegetarians. A mother gorilla in Rwanda (right). Gorilla mothers exhibit the nurturing behaviors towards their young of many primates.

© Paul Degrere/FPG International

MOUNTAIN GORILLA

Prior to the late 1970s, when researcher Dian Fossey established the Mountain Gorilla Project (MGP) in Rwanda, few people knew, or cared, much about the mountain gorilla. Today, the mountain gorilla is one of the more "popular" endangered species, and is at last receiving the protection and support it deserves.

Dian Fossey lived among the gorillas of the Volcanoes National Park in Rwanda for eighteen years. Her articles, which appeared on the pages of *National Geographic,* first introduced people around the world to the gentle, almost human nature of the gorilla.

Fossey and her staff fought long and hard to protect the gorillas from poachers—an effort that eventually cost Fossey her life. She was murdered, presumably by poachers, as she slept in her camp in December 1985.

The work of Dian Fossey continues in Rwanda through the Mountain Gorilla Project. The MGP today works closely with the Rwandan government to ensure the protection of gorillas by developing conservation education programs in the park, monitoring tourism so it does not interfere with the safety of the animals while habituating gorilla groups so tourist revenue continues, and maintaining a well-equipped and -trained anti-poaching force.

The Western image of the gorilla has always been that of a vicious killer, but the African people who have lived in the forests with the gorillas know these apes are peaceful vegetarians.

MOUNTAIN GORILLA

Gorilla gorilla berengei

Historical Range: Central and western Africa.

Current Range: Virunga Mountains of Rwanda and Zaire, and small forests in Uganda.

Estimated Wild Population: Less than 400.

Estimated Captive Population: In zoos around the world.

Major Threats: Poaching (for head trophies and gorilla-hand ashtrays) continues as a threat, though it has greatly decreased since the 1970s and 1980s. Habitat loss from clear-cutting forests. Disease can decimate already low populations.

Conservation Efforts: Continued anti-poaching campaign with well-armed and well-trained game wardens. Public education on gorilla and wildlife conservation and resource management. Education of tourists and control of tourist volume. Development of vaccines and medical care for gorillas.

Gorillas live in groups of three to about thirty animals, led by a dominant male, a few submissive males, females, and young. The action of a male gorilla beating its chest (so often portrayed in Hollywood) is accurate in that gorillas will drum their chests as a warning to other gorillas and, less often, toward intruders. Drumming may also serve as a form of communication to other groups.

While poaching has been the biggest threat to gorilla communities, they are also losing habitat from clear cutting of the native forests. Conservationists are working toward educating the native Rwandans on the importance of gorilla and other wildlife preservation, and sensible natural resource management.

A young gorilla (opposite page) dines on the tender shoots of bamboo, a staple food in its vegetarian diet. Although poaching has always been the major threat to their survival, clear-cutting of native forests is destroying gorilla habitats at an alarming rate.

SNOW LEOPARD

The Ounce, which was once thought to be but a longer-haired variety of the Leopard, is now known to be truly a separate species. The Ounce is an inhabitant of some parts of Asia, and specimens of this fine animal have been brought from the shores of the Persian Gulf.

—*THE NEW ILLUSTRATED NATURAL HISTORY*

Not much more than what was written above in the nineteenth century had been discovered about the "ounce," now called the snow leopard, until recently. It is one of the rarest of the big cats, and is also one of the least-studied of all endangered species.

A partial reason for the lack of studies of the snow leopard is its habitat—the remote and practically inaccessible Himalayan Mountains of Nepal. Until the organization of the Snow Leopard Project—a four-year field trip to Nepal (1981 to 1985)—no one had officially attempted to study the leopards in their own territory.

Biologist George Schaller had led a series of expeditions in the Himalayas during the 1970s and hoped he would be able to radio-collar the cats, but was unable to initiate the study at that time.

Above: The snow leopard's beautiful gray- and white-spotted coat makes it a target for poachers. Right: The snow leopard's home territory, the altitudes of the Himalaya Mountains, is shrinking under the pressure of human encroachment. These rare animals have not been able to adapt to life in any other habitat.

These leopards live above the tree line where few other predators venture. The leopards feed mostly on bharal, a mountain goat, but have been known to prey on livestock. Habitat loss and shooting by livestock owners are now the most serious threats to snow leopards.

SNOW LEOPARD

Panthera uncia

———

Historic Range: Central Asia.

Current Range: Mountains of India, Pakistan, Afghanistan, Nepal, Bhutan, Tibet, Mongolia, China, and parts of the Soviet Union.

Estimated Wild Population: There may be as many as 40,000.

Estimated Captive Population: Limited, in zoos.

Major Threats: Habitat loss; fragmented breeding populations; shooting by livestock owners and poachers.

Conservation Efforts: Education of mountain people and aid for those who have lost livestock to leopards. Protection of habitat. Continued study of leopard ecology.

Peter Matthiessen, who joined Schaller in Nepal and wrote *The Snow Leopard*, was no more successful in his attempts to observe the cat in its natural habitat.

Schaller's plan to capture and radio-collar snow leopards finally materialized through the efforts of the Snow Leopard Project originators, photographer/biologist Rod Jackson and Darla Hillard. Their book, *Vanishing Tracks*, gives the world new insight into the private lives of these magnificent animals.

The leopards live above the tree line, above the point where other predators venture. Their main source of food is the bharal, a type of mountain goat that clings to life on the cliffs, but they will eat whatever they can catch.

They are basically solitary animals but do share their space with other snow leopards. Space, lots of it, is required by the leopard to ensure its survival, and even in Nepal, that space is shrinking. Existing populations are becoming fragmented by human encroachment, making breeding difficult. Leopards are also killed when they overstep human "boundaries" by occasionally taking livestock.

The leopards face another danger—poaching of their fur—though this is no longer considered the major threat to their survival. It was in the recent past, however, a major factor in population declines.

FLORIDA MANATEE

Until recently the Florida manatee was thought to be the same as the West Indian manatee, but scientists have determined that this curious-looking creature is indeed a separate subspecies. In any case, both the Florida and West Indian manatees, which live in coastal waters from Florida to Guyana, are endangered species. Their West African cousins are listed as threatened.

Manatees are gentle creatures that resemble elephant seals, but have front flippers very near their necks. There are three nails on each flipper, used by the manatee to locate the vegetation on which it feeds. There are no rear flippers. Manatee heads are broad, with thick upper lips and soft, bristled muzzles.

They are sluggish, sociable animals that live in family groups, spending much of their daytime hours resting near the bottom, rising to the surface periodically to breathe. They forage for vegetation and small crustaceans at night.

The habitats of the manatee are the brackish, shallow waterways along the coast, areas that are also prime habitats for humans and their speedboats.

The massive body of a manatee just under the surface of coastal waters is difficult to see in time to avoid—especially when the boats are traveling at high speeds. Most manatees die from the impact or are seriously injured by propeller blades. Though some manatees are poached for their meat, Florida boaters pose the most serious threat to their survival.

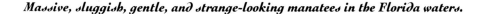

Massive, sluggish, gentle, and strange-looking manatees in the Florida waters.

FLORIDA MANATEE
Trichechus manatus latirostris

Historical Range: Coastal waters from the Carolinas south to the Florida Keys. The West Indian Manatee (*Trichechus manatus*) was found in waters south to Guyana.

Current Range: Coastal waters around Florida to the Keys; along the coast in Gulf of Mexico. The West Indian manatee ranges down to South America.

Estimated Wild Population: Minimum 1,200 in Florida waters; population in other areas unknown.

Estimated Captive Population: Approximately thirty.

Major Threats: Collisions with high-speed boats kill manatees and orphan calves, which then perish as well. Pollution of habitat: some animals ingest plastic bags and fish hooks; others become tangled in crab pot lines, which cut off circulation to their flippers. Some manatees are even poached, for meat.

Conservation Efforts: Implementation of public education and awareness programs to prevent reckless boat driving. Attempts to establish lower boating speed limits in coastal waters (currently opposed by the speedboat industry but supported by Florida boaters). Rehabilitation and release of injured manatees.

Manatees spend much time resting and feeding at the bottom of coastal waterways, surfacing periodically to breathe.

GIANT PANDA

The grizzly may be the most awesome bear, but its panda cousin is certainly the most loved. Pandas were virtually unknown to the Western world prior to 1869, but upon discovery of this curious bear, panda hunting expeditions were launched in the name of science. Teddy Roosevelt is credited with being the first Westerner to shoot a panda, in 1929, for the Chicago Field Museum of Natural History. The West didn't see a live panda until 1936, when Ruth Harkness brought home the cub, Soo-Lin. America's love affair with pandas was under way.

The world forgot about pandas in the years that followed, as the major countries moved through wars, isolation, political, and social changes. By the time things settled down and China had undergone a revolution of its own, nearly 100 animals had been shipped out of the country to different zoos and many more had been killed. In the 1970s the Chinese began field studies of the animals, in the mountainous bamboo forests of central China.

Realizing their pandas were in serious trouble, the Chinese government invited the World Wildlife Fund to join them in efforts to save the black-and-white bears.

As late as 1985, some controversy existed among biologists as to whether the panda was a bear at all or was more closely related to the raccoon. Panda paws are equipped with a flexible sixth digit that works like a thumb—a feature of the raccoon family. Pandas have black eye patches, don't roar (they bleat) or hibernate, eat bamboo almost exclusively, but have a carnivore's digestive system. The confusion has been cleared up by studying the animals' genetic history. Raccoons and bears, it was discovered, shared a common ancestor, but evolved so that today raccoons are raccoons and pandas are bears.

In an effort to preserve the giant panda's shrinking habitat, the Chinese government has set aside several panda reserves. In cooperation with the World Wildlife Fund, a panda preserve, research center, and captive breeding compound was built at Wolong, headquarters for the WWF/China Giant Panda Project. Zoos around the world are participating in panda breeding programs, but success has been minimal. Most of the cubs have died.

The most serious problem facing wild pandas is shrinking habitat, and an inability to move from one suitable area to another because of human habitation. Every seventy to eighty years, as part of its natural botanical cycle, umbrella bamboo (the staple of the panda's diet) flowers and dies. When this occurred during the late 1970s, about 150 pandas died of starvation because they could not relocate to new feeding areas. Isolated populations also face the danger of having too small a gene pool for healthy breeding. In addition, pandas are occasionally poached for their pelts. The Chinese government passed a law in 1987 imposing the death penalty on anyone convicted of killing a panda or selling its skin. In spite of this law, there is evidence that poaching has actually increased.

Pandas are receiving more help, possibly, than any other endangered species, but unless their habitats are sufficiently preserved, they may survive only as bears behind bars.

Pandas, the world's best-loved bear, are receiving more help than any other endangered species.

GIANT PANDA
Ailuropoda malanoleuca

———

Historical Range: Throughout central China.

Current Range: Wolong Reserve, Tangjiahe Reserve, small isolated populations in the Sichuan province, and southwest of Xi'an.

Estimated Wild Population: Approximately 1,000.

Estimated Captive Population: About ninety in China; about twenty-one as permanent residents in foreign zoos (diplomatic gifts from China), and about seven others on diplomatic short-term loans.

Major Threats: Loss of habitat and free movement due to encroaching human populations. Poaching for pelts (current Japanese black market price is $20,000). Wild populations are now too low for healthy breeding.

Conservation Efforts: Captive breeding programs, especially at Wolong, are working toward increasing the survival rates of cubs born in captivity. Efforts continue to preserve panda habitats and deter poaching. Ongoing studies of panda ecology.

Until recently, biologists wondered whether the giant panda was more of a raccoon than a bear, since it possesses many raccoon-like qualities. Another peculiarity: pandas feed almost exclusively on bamboo, even though they have a carnivorous digestive system.

A charging black rhino (above) is a beast to be reckoned with. Rhinos have been known to attack and overturn cars and trucks.

© Stan Osolinski/M.L. Dembinsky Photo Associates

RHINOCEROS

The earliest ancestors of the rhinoceros roamed over much of Europe and Africa some 12 million years ago. Today, five species of rhino survive: the black rhinoceros (*Diceros bicornis*) and the white rhinoceros (*Ceratotherium simum*) of Africa; the Indian rhino (*Rhinoceros unicornis*), the Sumatran rhino (*Dicerorhinus sumatrensis*), and the Javan rhino (*Rhinoceros sondaicus*), each found in Southeast Asia. All five are listed as endangered species.

In appearance, all rhinos look like they might be a cross between a pig, a prehistoric reptile, and an army tank. Thick, hairless skin covers a body longer than it is tall, solidly supported by four short legs that end abruptly with three hoofed toes on each foot. On some, particularly the Indian rhino, excess skin folds back on itself along the shoulders, hips, neck, and legs, giving the impression that the rhino is wearing a suit of armor. After the elephant, the white rhino and the black rhino are respectively the second and third largest of the earth's land mammals. An adult white rhino can reach an overall length of seventeen feet (5 m) and weigh in excess of three tons (2.7 t).

Rhinos have poor eyesight but keen hearing and sense of smell. They tend to charge moving objects they cannot readily identify, and have been known to attack and overturn cars and trucks. For the most part, however, they are peaceful, solitary animals that spend most of their adult lives foraging for the vegetation that is their staple diet, or wallowing in mud to cool their bodies, which lack sweat glands.

Rhinos' heads are elongated, large, and ponderous. The Indian rhino sports a single horn on the top of its nose; not as impressive as the double nose horns worn by the white, black, Sumatran, and Javan rhinos. Rhino horn is made of packed keratin, the same material that forms human fingernails. Rhinos use their horns to uproot vegetation, to break tree branches, to scrape out wallowing holes, as a formidable weapon when rhino tempers flare, and for other reasons only rhinos may know.

Humans have a different, more sinister, use for rhino horns. In the Middle East, the horns are used to make ceremonial dagger handles, which are prized status symbols. In the Orient, powdered rhinoceros horn is believed to cure fevers and headaches.

Although rhinos are protected under the Endangered Species Act, and although most governments have banned the importation of rhino horns by signing the CITES treaty, rhinos are continually slaughtered by poachers who risk being shot on sight for the riches the rhino horn brings on the black market. A recent black market price for a single horn averaged U.S. $4,500 (in 1985, the going price in Singapore was U.S. $5,000 a pound [.45 kg]).

For these reasons, in the last twenty years or so, the once-plentiful rhinoceros has been very nearly wiped from the face of the earth.

The white rhino also has been slaughtered for its horns. It has been estimated that only 15 individuals of the northern white rhino species remained in existence by the early 1980s. The northern rhino is found only in Zaire's Garamba National Park and in zoos. In the wild, the southern white rhino seems to be faring slightly better than its northern counterpart.

The Sumatran rhino inhabits the rain forests of Malay, Borneo, and Sumatra. It is the smallest of the rhinos, and most closely resembles its extinct prehistoric cousin that roamed Eurasia 12,000 years ago. Loss of rain forest habitat is the major reason for the decline of this species.

The Javan rhino also inhabits rain forests. Once found throughout India, Vietnam, Malay, and Indonesia, the Javan rhino exists today only in the densest rain forests of Java. Little is known of its habits; none are in captivity.

Indian rhinos are also victims of habitat loss. By the 1900s, development and exploding human populations had already pushed the Indian rhinos out of their habitats and within the reaches of extinction. Habitat loss, drought, and disease contribute to population declines, but poaching remains the most serious threat to African rhinos, occurring even within the boundaries of wildlife

Below: With its menacing-looking horn and body resembling a tank, the rhinoceros looks like a fierce animal. However, rhinos actually attack humans less frequently than is commonly believed.

© Thomas Henion

BLACK RHINOCEROS
Diceros bicornis

Historical Range: All of Africa south of the Sahara Desert (excluding equatorial rain forests).

Current Range: Small populations sparsely distributed throughout former range.

Estimated Wild Population: Less than 3,700.

Estimated Captive Population: Undetermined, although some zoos do have them.

Major Threats: Poaching: rhino horns are quickly sold on the black market for use in the Middle East and Orient. Habitat loss, drought, and disease are secondary to poaching. Breeding and reproduction cycles suffer from the low wild population.

Conservation Efforts: Wild rhinos are captured and relocated to the protective confines of fenced sanctuaries. Captive breeding programs sponsored by American Association of Zoological Parks and Aquariums (AAZPA) attempt to establish viable breeding populations of black rhinos (a "rhino bank," so to speak) so that rhinos could be released into former ranges when current survival and environmental threats have been reversed or are under control.

© Glenn Oliver/Visuals Unlimited

The magnificent horns of the rhino are sold on the black market to be made into dagger handles and used for medicinal and aphrodisiacal purposes.

refuges. In Kenya alone, a once-stable population of 20,000 black rhinos was reduced to 500 animals in less than ten years, although Kenya supports several national parks and wildlife refuges set aside specifically for rhino protection. To combat the poachers, Kenyan game wardens resorted to shooting poachers on sight.

High-voltage fencing has been erected around the perimeters of several African preserves in an effort to keep the animals in and the poachers out, and although the fencing restricts the natural migratory movements of many species within the parks, it also appears to be saving their lives. One fenced preserve was able to boast a full year without losing a rhino to a poacher.

Efforts to save the rhinos are now concentrating on relocating individual animals from high-risk areas to the safer confines of fenced sanctuaries and in establishing a captive breeding program that will eventually lead to the release of rhinos outside the sanctuary boundaries. It is hoped that the market for rhino horn will collapse when free-roaming rhinos become unavailable to poachers and that in the future, wild rhinos may again wander unrestricted across the African continent.

© Gerry Ellis/Ellis Wildlife Collection

BRAZILIAN THREE-TOED SLOTH

The Brazilian three-toed sloth spends its entire life in slow motion, suspended from the tree branches in the upper canopy of the Brazilian rain forest. It feeds solely on the cecropia plant, which makes maintaining sloths in captivity difficult. Its cousin, however, the two-toed sloth, tolerates a more varied diet and is the more common zoo sloth.

The three-toed sloth is named for the three scimitar-shaped claws on each foot that wrap securely around the vines and branches of the canopy, enabling the sloth to suspend itself above the forest floor. The sloth's arms are sufficiently long that every vine is within reach. A sloth without a branch to hang from can scarcely move at all.

Sloths are so adapted to hanging from trees that their fur grows in the opposite direction from most ground-dwelling mammals. The fur parts on the sloth's belly and hangs down toward its spine. Often the grayish fur is covered with microscopic plants, giving it a greenish tint and making the slow-moving sloth practically invisible in the treetops.

The three-toed sloth has been hunted by Brazilian natives for its meat—and was certainly one of the easiest animals to kill. The sloth is not capable of increasing its speed but attempts to frighten enemies by showing its black, enamelless teeth, or by wheezing. On occasion it will make a swing with its foreleg, attempting to use its sharp claws, but the "attack" is in slow-motion and therefore is never effective.

Sloths, like so many other Brazilian species, are losing their rain forest habitats at an alarming speed. This creature, so adapted to life in the rain forest canopy, simply cannot survive without those forests.

An entire lifetime spent in slow-motion! A Brazilian three-toed sloth is so at home in the treetops that it can hardly move at all on the ground.

WOLF

He (wolf) is particularly fond of human flesh; and, perhaps, if he was sufficiently powerful, he would eat no other.

—Buffon's *System of Natural History,* 1811

I give you Canis lupus. *Direct ancestor of every paper-fetching, car-chasing, bone-chewing, tail-wagging domestic dog alive today.*

—Bruce Thompson, *Looking at the Wolf*

It is possible to look closely at a stand of trees or through the swirling snow and not see the wolves. Your own hair tickles the back of your neck. A hint of yellow eye, a shadow of silent movement. The wolf is there! Or is he?

The wolf's phantomlike ability to silently fade in and out of its surroundings contributed to the notion that wolves were evil creatures that possessed supernatural powers. Their howling didn't help the situation.

Of all the sounds to be heard in nature, fewer evoke more emotion than the howl of a wolf. Depending on your point of view, the howl is the most beautiful and expressive natural sound you will ever hear or it will scare you half to death.

To the wolf, howling is a form of communication. Wolves howl to reassemble a scattered pack, to celebrate a hunt, to give warning to other wolves, to find each other during a storm. Wolves howl during courtship and mating, together or alone, and for reasons humans will never know.

To conservationists, the howl of a wolf is a symbol; it represents the wildness and open space that once echoed throughout the mountains and valleys of the northern hemisphere. It is a sound not heard in the wild for more than fifty years, except in parts of Alaska, Canada, and northern Minnesota, where stable populations of wolves survive.

Wolves are predators. Before Europeans came to North America, wolves preyed upon a variety of wildlife, from insects and mice to moose, caribou, and buffalo. For thousands of years, the wolf lived in balance with native animals and Native People, who called the wolf "Brother" and admired its skill as a hunter.

The European settlers felt no such respect for or harmony with the wolf. Of the estimated 500 million or more animals that died on America's plains (among them: passenger pigeons, buffalo, antelope, mustangs, coyotes, and grizzlies), none was treated as savagely as the wolf.

Wolves were shot, trapped, and poisoned. Dens with cubs inside were dynamited, cubs were clubbed or choked to death. Trapped alive, wolves suffered unspeakably at the hands of their captors. Government agencies offered bounties for wolf carcasses, and in 1915 passed a law allowing wolf extermination on federal lands, including national parks. By the time this "wolf control"

Opposite page: The phantom-like silence of a pack of timber wolves once gave people the notion that wolves were supernatural and evil beings. This timber wolf (above) enjoys a nap after a feast on a deer carcass.

MEXICAN WOLF

Canis lupus baileyi

Historic Range: Mexico, southeastern Arizona, southwestern New Mexico, southern Texas.

Current Range: Virtually extinct in the wild.

Estimated Wild Population: Less than fifty in Mexico as of 1981. The last Mexican wolves in Texas, Arizona, and New Mexico were killed by 1976.

Estimated Captive Population: There are several breeding facilities, among them the Wild Canid Survival and Research Center in Missouri, which breeds the Mexican wolves for the U.S. Fish and Wildlife Service, the St. Louis Zoo, and the Rio Grande Zoo in Albuquerque, New Mexico.

Major Threats: Habitat loss. Wild population too low for healthy reproduction. Continued persecution by humans.

Conservation Efforts: Conservationists are attempting to secure approval for release sites. The U.S. Department of Defense denied an application for the release of Mexican wolves on the White Sands Missile Base in New Mexico, a prime location. Feasibility studies for the Gila/Leopold Wildlands Complex in New Mexico were also refused. The captive wolves are in danger of becoming too domesticated to survive in the wild before a suitable site is located. They may survive only as captive animals.

Less than 50 Mexican wolves survive in the wild. Captive-bred animals await a government-approved release site.

program was terminated in the 1940s, the gray wolf had been effectively exterminated from its former ranges in North America. Several subspecies were extinct.

Preservation efforts today center on the gray wolf, *Canis lupus*; and two subspecies, the eastern timber wolf, *Canis lupus lycaon*, and Mexican wolf, *Canis lupus baileyi*; and on the red wolf, *Canis rufus*.

Only recently have biologists attempted to study the living wolf. They have learned that the wolf is not responsible for population declines in big game species, but rather, wolves naturally manage the numbers of these species by filling an important niche in the predator/prey relationship. They have learned that wolves are intelligent, highly social, and basically timid animals that prefer to range far from the human species. There are no documented cases of healthy, wild wolves attacking humans.

Wolf Recovery Plans, developed and managed by the U.S. Fish and Wildlife Service, designed to reintroduce the gray wolf to former ranges in the western United States, including the Rocky Mountains and Yellowstone National Park, have met with opposition from ranchers and hunters, who are still concerned about the safety of their livestock and game animals.

© H.G. Ross/FPG International

RED WOLF

Canis rufus

Historical Range: Southeastern United States, from the Carolinas to southern Missouri, Oklahoma, and Texas.

Current Range: Biologically extinct in the wild. An introduced population exists in Alligator River Refuge, North Carolina.

Estimated Wild Population: Released: less than twenty.

Estimated Captive Population: Less than 100.

Major Threats: Habitat loss, persecution, harsh environment. Their population decreased to the point where red wolves began breeding with coyotes and feral dogs; now pure red wolves are almost impossible to identify.

Conservation Efforts: Wild red wolves were captured to determine their purity of species and stop hybridization. Captive-bred wolves have been released in Alligator River National Wildlife Refuge, North Carolina, and Bull's Island in Cape Romain National Wildlife Refuge, South Carolina. Several of the released animals have since died, but some cubs have been born and survived. Biologists have determined that the wild population must reach at least 200, and an additional 300 animals must remain in captive breeding to maintain genetic diversity.

Red wolves are biologically extinct, and attempts at releasing captive-bred animals in the wild have met with limited success.

© Gerry Ellis/Ellis Wildlife Collection

GRAY WOLF

Canis lupus

Historical Range: All of North America, excluding the southeastern states; parts of Mexico.

Current Range: Twelve gray wolves migrated from British Columbia to northern Montana in 1985. A small pack remains in that region; sightings have been reported in Idaho. Populations stable in Alaska and Canada.

Estimated Wild Population: Population in Alaska estimated at less than 5,000; there may be up to 7,000 in Canada.

Estimated Captive Population: In zoos and in a few wolf sanctuaries for behavior study and captive breeding.

Major Threats: Loss of habitat: wolves require extensive territory free of human encroachment. Illegal hunting and trapping due to misconceptions and fear.

Conservation Efforts: The Wolf Recovery Plan has three recovery sites under consideration for reintroduction of the gray wolf: northwestern Montana, including Glacier National Park; central Idaho, where there have been limited sightings; and Yellowstone National Park.

Apparently, antiquated habits and superstitions are difficult to change. One big-game hunter, commenting in a national hunting magazine on the plan to reintroduce wolves to Yellowstone, wrote "this is the biggest anti-hunting scheme I've ever come across." The hunter is concerned that the wolves will decimate the herds, leaving no big-game targets for his paying customers.

Although protected by the ESA in the lower forty-eight states, wolves are still hunted by airplane in Alaska. Wolfers may not shoot from the plane; they chase until the wolves are exhausted, land the plane, and shoot their defenseless prey on the ground. In Minnesota, an estimated one-quarter of the surviving population is illegally slaughtered each year by ignorant, hysterical people.

Is it the wolf that humans hate—or do they hate that part of themselves that they see in the wolf? Which one is the more dangerous animal?

Wolves are fascinating creatures. They hunt at night, and can reach speeds of up to 40 to 50 miles per hour (64 to 80 km) when in pursuit of their prey. Wolves mate for life, just one example of their developed social structure.

EASTERN TIMBER WOLF

Canis lupus lycaon

Historical Range: North America, from Minnesota south to eastern Tennessee, Georgia, and Florida.

Current Range: Northern Minnesota, parts of Wisconsin, Isle Royale in Lake Superior.

Estimated Wild Population: Approximately 1,200 in Minnesota; 25 in Wisconsin; 25 on Isle Royale.

Estimated Captive Population: In zoos and wolf sanctuaries.

Major Threats: Habitat loss. Illegal hunting and trapping. Wolves on Isle Royale were recently decimated by a disease thought to be parvovirus, an infectious canine disease discovered in domestic dogs in 1977. Parvovirus was most likely transported to Isle Royale on the clothing and belongings of human visitors.

Conservation Efforts: Conservationist groups are working to educate the public on the true nature of wolves. Efforts exist to ensure protection of existing populations.

© Pieter Folkens

VAQUITA
(Also known as Gulf of California Harbor Porpoise, or Cochito)

The rarest member of the cetacean family was unknown to science prior to 1958, when an unidentifiable porpoise skull was found on the beach near San Felipe, on the upper portion of the Gulf of California. Scientists named the discovery *Phocoena sinus* (*sinus* is the Latin word for "bay"), and although it was a new species for them, Mexican fishermen had observed the small porpoise for years. To them, it was the "little cow," vaquita. Others called it *cochito*.

By whatever name it is known, this small porpoise has proved to be much more elusive than other porpoises and dolphins. Observations of living animals have been fleeting at best, and most of what we know of the vaquita has come, unfortunately, from studying dead bodies.

In 1985, seven vaquitas were caught in gill nets being used by Mexican fishermen to catch totoabas (a species of large sea bass), the major commercial species. A member of the Mexican national fisheries ministry, Alejandro Robles, sent out with the fishermen in order to research declining populations of totoabas, recognized the dead vaquitas as the first intact specimens of this porpoise ever seen. He placed the animals in the ship's freezer, wrapped one in newspaper, and hand-delivered it to the Monterrey Institute Department of Marine Sciences, a 500-mile (800-kg) journey. Scientists had their first look at a whole vaquita.

From these and additional specimens inadvertently killed in gill nets, scientists determined most of what we now know about the vaquitas: maximum length is about five feet (1.5 m), weight about 100 pounds (45 kg), making them the smallest cetaceans. For their size, their dorsal fins are larger than those of any other porpoise. In color, the vaquitas are similar to other porpoises, but have dark eye patches.

We know virtually nothing at all about their natural history or everyday life. We do know that we nearly lost them before we ever found them.

Continued use of gill nets and drift nets are the major threat to the vaquitas, but degradation of their habitat is also a factor. The entire population of vaquitas, whatever that number might be, live solely in the upper part of the Gulf of California, which is suffering from organochlorine pollutants and chemical contaminants.

The Colorado River once cascaded into the gulf, adding nutrients to the water. Diverted by a dam, the once-mighty waters of the Colorado now only trickle into the gulf. The natural cleansing action of the river has ceased, allowing the organic and chemical contamination to increase.

Although the vaquita is recognized as an endangered species in the United States, the porpoise lives solely in Mexican waters. Its survival will depend on cooperation between the United States, Mexico, and the fishermen of the gulf.

The vaquita is so rarely seen that biologists know very little about this smallest member of the porpoise family. Indeed, it only came to scientific attention when the remains of a dead vaquita were found in 1958.

RIGHT WHALE

So named because they were considered by early whalers as the "right" whale to kill, the northern and southern right whales have never really recovered from the whalers' uncontrolled slaughter and are today probably the most endangered of all the great whales.

Right whales were favored by whalers because, in addition to the meat, oil, and other products the whale provided, right whales moved more slowly than other whales, making them easier to pursue from the man-powered, primitive whaling boats. The high concentration of oil in their bodies caused the whales to float after they were killed, and so right whales were easier than other species to locate and process.

© Marty Snyderman/Visuals Unlimited

At left, a southern right whale cow swims with its calf. In close-up (above, left) the right whale's large head and eye. This page, a diver swims alongside a right whale.

Right whales are among the Mysticete or baleen whales, which have no teeth and feed on plankton and other small organisms that the whale strains from the ocean waters through a series of plates, or baleen, that grow down from the upper jaws in its mouth. In contrast, the Odontoceti, or toothed whales, prey on smaller species using their teeth and jaws, much like any other predator.

Baleen was a valuable by-product of the whale. It was used in the manufacture of many articles that are now made of plastic.

Right whales are classified as the northern right whale (*Eubalaena glacialis*), which inhabits the waters of the northern hemisphere, and the southern right whale (*Eubalaena australis*), which inhabits the southern Atlantic, Pacific, and Indian oceans. They are identical in appearance, and geographical distribution seems to be the only difference in the two species. Thus, many biologists believe that the two should not be classified separately.

Right whales are usually black in color, with white patches on their chins and bellies. Their enormous mouths and heads account for about 30 percent of their overall body length, which averages forty-five to fifty-three feet (14 to 16 m).

RIGHT WHALE

(*Eubalaena glacialis* and *Eubalaena australis*)

Historic Range: Oceans of the northern and southern hemispheres.

Current Range: *E. glacialis:* north Atlantic and north Pacific oceans, from Greenland to Florida, Gulf of Mexico, Azores and Northwest Africa in the Atlantic to the Gulf of Alaska south to Taiwan and the Gulf of California in the Pacific.

E. australis: Brazil and South Africa south to Patagonia in Atlantic/southern ocean; Australia, New Zealand and south Indian Ocean.

Estimated Wild Population: *E. glacialis:* approximately 200 to 500.

E. australis: approximately 3,000.

Estimated Captive Population: None.

Major Threats: Populations have been so seriously decreased by commercial whaling that natural recovery may not be possible. Toxic chemicals and oil pollution of ocean water threaten the habitat, as do commercial marine traffic and human disturbance.

Sea and river otters wear the most luxurious of furs, which protect them from the frigid temperatures of icy waters.

RIVER AND SEA OTTERS

Otters are members of the weasel family, and like their weasel cousins, otters tend to keep a low profile in the wild. The otter's secretive nature makes it difficult to observe the animal for extended periods of time, but any encounter with an otter is sure to be entertaining.

The short legs, arched back, and thick, tapered tail that look so cumbersome and out of place on land transform the otter into an underwater torpedo with the agility to overtake the quickest fish.

The otter's legs and webbed feet act as rudders and swim fins, while its muscular tail provides propulsion. Thick, oily fur keeps water away from the otter's body, making the animal immune to frigid temperatures. Otters are among the few animals that are not adversely affected by winter weather. In fact, they actually seem to enjoy it.

Give an otter a snow-covered embankment leading down to the water, and he'll turn it into a playground by running up the embankment and belly-flopping down.

Otter pelts are among the most luxurious, and the otters have paid dearly for having such warm, thick fur; due to the demand for coats made of their fur, most species of freshwater and sea otters are now endangered.

Among these are the southern river otter (*Lutra provocax*), an animal whose distribution is confined to southern and central Chile and Argentina. We know very little about this particular otter's natural history or present status, but it is believed that their numbers have declined drastically due to fur trapping.

Another endangered otter is the giant otter (*Pteronura brasiliensis*), native to South America. This impressive animal can attain an overall length of 7.5 feet (2 m), from nose tip to tail tip. This provides a profitable amount of fur. More than 7,000 hides were legally exported from Brazil alone during a fifteen-year period. This does not take into account the number of smuggled pelts.

The southern sea otter (*Enhydra lutris nereis*), commonly known as the California sea otter, is one species that seems to have made a slight recovery. It was believed extinct by the early 1920s, but a small population of sea otters was discovered during the latter part of the 1930s, and today it is estimated that less than 1,800 survive.

The California sea otter is found in Monterey Bay and along the southern coast of California. Here, the otter is the subject of controversy between the shellfish industries, which see the otter and its appetite as a major threat to future profits, and environmentalists, who argue that the otter is a natural resident of the California coastline and entitled to remain in its habitat.

Although otters consume about one-quarter of their body weight in shellfish every day, the shellfish industries' habit of overharvesting presents a greater threat to the number of shellfish.

SEA OTTER

Enhydra lutris nereis

Historic Range: West coast of the United States, south of Mexico.

Current Range: Scattered populations within former ranges.

Estimated Wild Population: Approximately 1,800.

Estimated Captive Population: Unavailable.

Major Threats: The fur trade decimated otter populations historically; today, persecution from the shellfish industries, drift-net fishing, and oil spills threaten them. Long-term effects of spills such as the *Exxon Valdez* are unknown.

Conservation Efforts: Compromises are being sought to accommodate the shellfish industry while protecting the otter's niche in the ecosystem; some benefits may come from ongoing conservation efforts related to offshore drilling and oil pollution. The sea otter is protected in all areas in United States jurisdiction. It is classified as a threatened, not endangered, species.

Populations of sea otters were relatively low before the disastrous oil spill of the **Exxon Valdez.** *What long term effects the spill will have on the otters is unknown.*

© Jeff Foott/Valan Photos

ENDANGERED BIRDS

MACAWS

The tropical regions of the planet are home to the most diverse and abundant wildlife species. According to the *ICBP Red Data Book,* 43 percent of the world's threatened and endangered birds live in tropical forests.

Many birds of the parrot family are familiar to people around the world who have never set foot in a tropical forest because of the popularity of these birds as caged pets. From budgerigars of Australia to the largest of macaws, parrots and parrotlike species are a favorite, and often quite expensive, exotic pet.

Much controversy surrounds the cage-bird industry. Avid birdwatchers condemn the practice of taking exotic birds as pets, and there is no doubt that many avian lives have been lost in the process of satisfying the market. Accounts of both legal and illegal trade in exotic species are rife with horror stories. Even officially protected species are not really protected, since bird trappers will risk being caught in order to collect as much as $20,000 for a single parrot.

Today, most pets are captive-bred birds, and aviculturists contribute research, knowledge, and public education to help protect exotic species in their natural habitats. Dealing in wild-caught species is discouraged, but as long as there is a pet bird market, the trade in illegally obtained birds will persist.

Exotic parrots, like the great green macaw, face other dangers besides the bird trappers. The same bird that might bring thousands of dollars in the bird-trade market is often unceremoniously shot, plucked, and eaten in its native land.

Some endangered parrot species are very similar in appearance to species that are still fairly common, and illegal activities involving these birds sometimes inadvertently escape detection by law-enforcement officers and bird dealers alike. The similar species include the highly endangered Guayaquil great green macaw, the great green macaw, also endangered, and the military macaw, which is much more common.

Although the pet-bird industry remains a danger to exotic parrot survival, according to the *ICBN Red Data Book,* international trade in exotic birds accounts for only 9 percent of the principal threats to bird life, while habitat destruction accounts for 60 percent; hunting 29 percent; and competition from introduced species, 20 percent.

There is a brisk international trade in exotic birds with showy plumage, such as this red and green macaw.

© Gary Randall/FPG International

GUAYAQUIL GREAT GREEN MACAW

Ara ambigua guayaquilensis

———

Historic Range: Tropical Central and South America.

Current Range: Lowland rain forests of southern central and northwestern South America. The Guayaquil great green macaw is the southern cousin of the great green macaw (also called Buffon's macaw), and is probably now restricted to the Chongon Hills of western Ecuador.

Estimated Wild Population: Exact wild population numbers are unknown; termed "very scarce" by most sources.

Estimated Captive Population: Undetermined.

Major Threats: Popularity as pets; rapid and total habitat destruction; low breeding output; local hunting for food and feathers.

Conservation Efforts: Restrictions (and enforcement) of international trade, public education, habitat preservation.

An Ecuadorian cousin of the great green macaw (pictured here), the Guayaquil great green macaw is losing its fight for survival as its rain forest habitat is rapidly destroyed.

CRESTED HONEYCREEPER
(Hawaiian name: 'Akohekohe')

© Todd G. Telander

Above: *The crested honeycreeper.* Opposite page: *This color-ful Hawaiian honeycreeper may not survive if the development of its Hawaiian habitat continues.*

CRESTED HONEYCREEPER

Palmeria dolei

Historical Range: Molokai and Maui.

Current Range: Narrow belt of rain forest on Haleakala Volcano, Maui. Extinct on Molokai.

Estimated Wild Population: In the early 1980s, it was estimated that between 700 and 3,800 crested honeycreepers remained in the wild.

Estimated Captive Population: None.

Major Threats: Destruction of habitat by feral pigs and human habitation.

Conservation Efforts: Hawaii is attempting to control feral pig populations and to protect the remaining undisturbed forest habitats.

The greatest concentration of the world's endangered birds is located in the Hawaiian Islands, the most isolated landmasses on the planet. This isolation from the rest of the world has enabled Hawaiian wildlife to evolve in its own particular way, and there are species found there that exist nowhere else in the world. Unique species have developed on other, similarly isolated islands like the Galapagos, Australia, and New Zealand.

Hawaii's undisturbed landscape of rugged volcanic mountains and rich rain forests in a tropical climate once exploded with animal and bird life, but the islands' flora and fauna have never recovered from their discovery by the outside world, about 1,500 years ago. Polynesian rats were introduced to the islands by settlers, and Europeans later brought black rats. Cats and mongooses were introduced to combat the rats. Pigs escaped to run wild in the forests, becoming feral, and uprooting sensitive vegetation. Caged birds brought a host of avian diseases that the delicate native species were unable to resist. Alien plants added to the mayhem.

Many of Hawaii's honeycreepers were killed by Polynesian settlers who used the brightly colored feathers to make cloaks for Hawaiian kings. The birds were also used for food. It is estimated that perhaps more than half of Hawaii's native birds were hunted to extinction even before the arrival of the European settlers. More recently, honeycreepers have been adversely affected by the clearing of lowland forests for pineapple and sugarcane crops.

Today, the Hawaiian Islands have the appearance of a tropical paradise, but to many native species, especially the honeycreepers, paradise isn't what it used to be. The biggest threats facing already dangerously low populations of these birds come from the devastation to vegetation caused by feral pigs, and from human interference and development of the islands.

Honeycreepers are a good example of adaptive radiation, an evolutionary process by which populations establish themselves in new areas, adapt to environmental conditions, and evolve into new species. The 16 genera, 28 species, and 18 subspecies of Hawaiian honeycreepers are found nowhere else in the world. Although all the honeycreepers belong to the same family, each individual species has adapted physically to different ecological niches. Some honeycreepers have long, down-curved bills for extracting nectar from flowers; others have bills suited for crushing seeds, and still others have a bill similar to that of a woodpecker, designed for removing insects from tree bark.

Other Endangered Hawaiian Honeycreepers:

Akepa, Hawaii (*Loxops coccineus coccineus*)

Akepa, Maui (*Loxops coccineus ochraceus*)

Akialoa, Kauai (*Hemignathus procerus*)

Akiapolaau (*Hemignathus munroi*)

Finch, Laysan (*Telespyza cantans*)

Finch, Nihoa (*Telespyza ultima*)

Nukupu'u (*Hemignathus lucidus*)

O'o (*Psittirostra psittacea*)

Palila (*Loxioides bailleui*)

Maui Parrotbill (*Pseudonestor xanthophrys*)

Po'ouli (*Melamprosops phaeosoma*)

Assorted toxins, lead poisoning, and shrinking habitats have eliminated all California condors in the wild. The only surviving birds are in captivity.

CALIFORNIA CONDOR

The California condor is probably the best-known example of a species whose survival depends on successful captive breeding.

Condors once soared over much of the southern United States, from California to Florida, and north into British Columbia. Their ancestry can be traced to the Pleistocene Ice Ages. But as early as the 1940s, less than 100 condors survived, in a small area of the California mountains. By 1983 their numbers had dropped to approximately 20. In 1987, the last three wild condors were captured and taken into "protective custody."

What happened to cause the near extinction of a bird that has been around since the ice ages? Condors are vultures—birds that feed on carrion. Studies of dead condors have indicated the highest level of toxins found in any land birds, including especially high levels of lead.

Lead shot used by hunters contaminated the game carcasses the condors fed upon. In addition, condors also ate the poisoned bait carcasses ranchers and farmers set for predators.

As a result, the condors are now doomed to extinction, or existence only as a zoo animal, unless a condor preserve can be established that will include enough poison-free land and food to support a wild population. Since condors habitually fly far over their mountainous territories in search of food, what exactly would constitute "enough" poison-free land is subject to debate.

In the meantime, science has proven that we can keep condors alive and breeding in captivity. The question is, can we also keep them alive and breeding in the wild?

CALIFORNIA CONDOR
Gymnogyps californianus

———

Historic Range: From British Columbia and California, south and east to Florida.

Current Range: Until 1987, the mountains of southern California.

Estimated Wild Population: None.

Estimated Captive Population: Approximately thirty-one.

Major Threats: Poisoning from lead and predator-control substances.

Conservation Efforts: All remaining condors are in captive-breeding programs. Release into the wild depends on cost of suitable land and the ability to maintain and manage a poison-free condor preserve. Experts acknowledge problems with knowledge of condor biology and ecology and maintaining condors in captivity.

Captive-bred condors cannot be released until a totally poison-free environment can be established and maintained.

ABBOTT'S BOOBY

Yes, there are birds called "boobies," lots of them. As of this writing, only the Abbott's booby is officially listed as endangered.

Boobies were so named because of their unusual tameness, which early settlers attributed to extreme stupidity. Boobies could be approached by predators and people, and were easy prey for both. Sailors clubbed them for food.

Guano miners on Assumption Island wiped out the entire colony of boobies there by the 1940s. The Abbott's booby once inhabited many of the islands near Madagascar, but the only known colony today is on Christmas Island.

Boobies are tropical ocean birds (gannets are the northern cousins of the boobies) that fish by diving, catching, and holding fish with their large, razor-sharp, saw-toothed bills.

Although it is estimated that boobies may live for twenty years or more, beginning life as an Abbott's booby is extremely hazardous: chicks take nearly eight months to develop to the point that they are independent of their parents. Being very subdued in character, many chicks are taken by predators long before they reach maturity. The survival rate of Abbott's booby chicks is estimated at less than 10 percent—certainly a contributing factor to their population decline.

Another threat to the remaining boobies is the fact that, unlike other boobies and gannets that nest on the ground, the Abbott's booby prefers to nest in the tall trees on Christmas Island—trees that have been clear-cut to expose the phosphate-rich soil underneath to phosphate miners.

In 1980 a national park was created on Christmas Island in an effort to preserve the Abbott's booby, as well as many other wildlife species that are found there. Forests are cut more selectively now, but cut nevertheless.

Other endemic birds on Christmas Island known to be endangered are Andrew's frigatebird (*Fregata andrewsi*) and the Christmas Island goshawk (*Accipiter fasciatus natalis*).

Because of their unusual tameness, early explorers and settlers thought that these birds were extremely stupid and so named them "boobies." In fact, the birds are simply good-natured. Pictured are the blue-footed booby (right) and red-footed booby (page 92).

ABBOTT'S BOOBY
Sula abbotti

———

Historic Range: Islands north and east of Madagascar.

Current Range: Christmas Island in the Indian Ocean.

Estimated Wild Population: No more than 2,000 breeding pairs.

Estimated Captive Population: Undetermined.

Major Threats: Loss of nesting habitat due to cutting of rain forest for phosphate mining. Low breeding success ratios.

Conservation Efforts: Rain forest protection. Creation of a national park on Christmas Island to preserve habitats.

ESKIMO CURLEW

This once-abundant shorebird, called a "doughbird" because of the extra layer of fat the bird built up for winter migration, is all but extinct. During the late 1800s, Eskimo curlews were also called "prairie pigeons," an analogy to the passenger pigeon flocks that "darkened the skies" with their numbers. Curlews proved to be easy targets—slow to take flight and quick to land again—and the birds could be shot by the hundreds. Passenger pigeons were hunted to extinction; the Eskimo curlew came dangerously close to the same fate.

Environmental factors also contributed to the drastic decline in the Eskimo curlew population. The birds once bred in the Arctic tundra of the Northwest Territories of Canada, wintering on the pampas grasslands of Argentina. When the Argentine grasslands began to be cultivated during the late 1800s, the curlews were left without wintering grounds. Their northward migration took them across the western prairies, where they were shot en masse during their spring and fall migrations.

This destructive combination was more than the curlew population could withstand, and by the early 1900s, most of the curlews had disappeared.

Today, the only known breeding ground of the Eskimo curlew is in the northwest Canadian arctic.

ESKIMO CURLEW
(Numenius borealis)

Historic Range: Arctic tundra and Canadian Northwest Territories to Argentina.

Current Range: Only known breeding occurs in the Canadian arctic.

Estimated Wild Population: There may be about twenty birds left, although some estimators believe the Eskimo curlew to be extinct.

Estimated Captive Population: None.

Major Threats: Hunting to brink of extinction and loss of breeding/wintering grounds has possibly resulted in the population becoming too low to recover.

Conservation Efforts: Protected in Canada and the United States under ESA.

The Eskimo curlew may already be extinct, due to a disastrous combination of ruthless hunting and habitat destruction.

DALMATIAN PELICAN

Pelicans are among the world's most curious-looking birds and are a species that most people can recognize instantly, even if they know nothing about bird identification.

The pelican's short, squat stature and enormous beak, with its floppy pouch, brings instant recognition.

Of the several species of pelicans, the Dalmatian pelicans of southeastern Europe, and the brown pelican of the southern United States, West Indies, and South America are the most endangered.

Pelicans may be interesting and unique in the eyes of nature lovers and birdwatchers, but commercial fishermen see the birds as competition that must be eliminated.

A Dalmatian pelican (below and right) uses its massive beak to preen feathers. It is one of the most endangered birds, with less than 1,300 breeding pairs surviving worldwide.

© Robert & Linda Mitchell

Pelicans feed by scooping fish from the water with their huge beaks, either while swimming on the surface or dropping from the air, beak first, into an unsuspecting school of fish.

Millions of Dalmatian pelicans inhabited most of Europe and Russia, Turkey, Iran, and Romania at the turn of the century. Today it is estimated that there are fewer than 1,300 breeding pairs left in the world.

Pelicans have been killed not only for being fishing competition, but also for food. In addition, their pouch skin has been used as a leather substitute for a variety of handmade items.

Habitat destruction has also contributed to the decline of the Dalmatian pelican; the birds nest in wetlands that are drained for agricultural purposes.

DALMATIAN PELICAN

(Pelecanus crispus)

Historic Range: Europe, Russia, Romania, Greece, Turkey.

Current Range: Greatest number exist in the Balkan region of southeastern Europe.

Estimated Wild Population: No more than 1,300 breeding pairs worldwide.

Estimated Captive Population: Unknown.

Major Threats: Breeding habitat loss; commercial fishing nets entangle some birds; persecution and destruction of nesting sites; floods during breeding periods and predation of nestlings.

Conservation Efforts: Protected in Russia, Romania, Bulgaria, Yugoslavia, Greece, and Turkey.

Brown pelicans (below and right), with their unusual color and distinctive bill, are among the most easily recognized species. Pelicans are magnificent divers; they plunge into the water and use their pouched bills to scoop up fish.

© Jeff Foott

© Robert & Linda Mitchell

© Fred Bavendam/Valan Photos

SIBERIAN WHITE CRANE

The plight of this once-abundant, regal-looking bird succeeded in breaking through diplomatic barriers, bringing the United States and the Soviet Union together in a cooperative effort to save the birds from extinction.

The International Crane Foundation, headquartered in Washington, D.C., receives eggs collected from breeding colonies in Siberia, which are flown to Moscow and then to the United States.

The Siberian is the largest of the cranes, distinguished both by its size and its scarlet-colored face. The North American cousin of the Siberian crane is the whooping crane, which was once a common sight throughout the plains and wetlands of the United States and Canada. By the early 1940s, only twenty-one of these birds could be counted.

Whooping cranes were shot, mostly for feathers to adorn ladies' hats, but were also affected by the loss of breeding grounds, which were drained and cultivated during the late 1800s and early 1900s. By the late 1980s, about 100 whooping cranes remained.

In America, the whooping crane is a symbol for conservation efforts. Attempts to breed the cranes in captivity have met with some success, but progress is slow. Another cousin, the Sandhill crane, has proved to be a successful foster-parent species for transplanted whooping crane eggs, and the focus for conservation programs is on establishing a stable whooping crane population with the help of the Sandhill cranes.

The plight of the majestic Siberian white crane prompted the United States and the Soviet Union to join forces in an effort to increase crane populations by using common cranes as foster parents.

MAURITIUS KESTREL

Falco punctatus

Historic Range: Mauritius Island.

Current Range: Same.

Estimated Wild Population: Dropped from "plentiful" in the 1850s to less than ten birds counted in early 1970s. A more thorough search in 1985 put the kestrel population at around fifty.

Estimated Captive Population: Ten individuals in a captive-breeding program as of 1983. Numbers fluctuate due to high mortality rates.

Major Threats: Loss of habitat; predation by rats, monkeys, and man. Pesticide poisoning. Population may be too low to sustain reproduction.

Conservation Efforts: Captive breeding. Establishment of Jersey Wildlife Preservation Trust working with government to establish and maintain public education and to preserve existing habitats.

MAURITIUS KESTREL

This small kestrel is among the world's rarest birds of prey. Once abundant in Mauritius, one of three islands off the eastern coast of Africa and Madagascar, the kestrel was described as plentiful throughout indigenous forests. Mauritius was once covered with dense, tropical foliage, which has since been almost totally stripped, burned, and transformed into grazing fields for pigs and cattle.

The remaining population of kestrels survives only in the deep mountain gorges where native forests are relatively undisturbed. There are factors other than habitat destruction that are taking their toll on this small predator. Introduced species, especially mynah birds and red-whiskered bulbuls, feed on the same food source as the kestrel: primarily the gecko, a small lizard.

Pesticide poisoning from the polluted farmlands below has affected the kestrel's breeding and hatching success. Rats and monkeys prey on young birds. Hunters shoot the kestrels, believing they prey on domestic poultry. It is a wonder that any birds survive.

Some kestrels have been successfully captive-bred, but unless the habitat is preserved the kestrel will most likely follow in the footsteps of another victim late of Mauritius—the dodo.

One of the world's rarest birds is the small Mauritius kestrel. Clear-cutting of the kestrel's forest habitat to provide grazing land for sheep and pigs has eliminated their suitable breeding grounds.

ENDANGERED REPTILES

AMERICAN CROCODILE

Though probably not on everyone's list of favorite animals, the American crocodile is nevertheless one of the most respected. A full-grown crocodile has more than 100 razor-sharp teeth in an elongated mouth capable of seizing a fairly large animal—including a human—though humans are not a croc's favorite food.

It is the teeth of the crocodile that most easily distinguish it from its cousin, the alligator: the large, grasping teeth at the front of the jaw are exposed when a croc's mouth is closed, while those of the alligator are hidden from view in the bony pits of the upper jaw.

Crocodiles, alligators, caimans, and the gharial are the species that make up the order *crocodilia*. They are reptiles—among the largest and most dangerous in the world. They have changed little from their prehistoric beginnings; in fact, crocodiles are the last living link to their prehistoric ancestors. And bizarre as it sounds, science has determined that they are the nearest living relatives to birds.

There are several species of crocodile. Some have attained lengths of about thirty feet (9 m), but an overall length of twenty feet (6 m) is more common.

Crocs in captivity have lived more than forty years, but studies of the Nile crocodile suggest that these animals may live well over 100 years in their natural habitats.

Most crocodiles inhabit tropical swamps and waterways, especially in Africa, southeast Asia, Mexico, and South America. The American crocodile lives in the coastal estuaries, lagoons, and swamps throughout its range.

Wherever they live, the survival of the crocodile species is in jeopardy; most are close to extinction. Crocs have been killed by the thousands for their skins, which are fashioned into shoes, belts, handbags, luggage, and other luxuries. They are killed also for sport and to a lesser degree, because of their predation on livestock, chiefly cattle, that venture into their waters.

Interestingly, the population of Nile crocodiles has decreased to such an extent that the number of Nile catfish, the croc's major meal, increased dramatically. The catfish feed on the same fish species favored by humans. In an attempt to rectify the situation, crocodiles are now raised in captivity and released on the Nile.

Despite their ferocious looks, crocodiles are relatively docile creatures and prefer to keep away from humans when given the choice. Fishermen in Haiti and the Dominican Republic regularly wade through crocodile-infested waters without mishap.

Although protected by law in the United States and the Dominican Republic, crocodiles are still killed for their meat and hides. In Haiti, there are no protective laws for crocodiles. Wherever they live, the greatest threat the crocodiles face is the contamination and loss of their wetland habitats.

Crocodiles have changed little in appearance from their prehistoric ancestors. They are among the world's largest and most dangerous reptiles, but at the same time are relatively docile and prefer to avoid human contact.

© Jeff Foott

Young crocodiles were often sold as pets, an arrangement that seldom lasted very long, and many others were sold as stuffed souvenirs of a visit to the southern states. Probably fewer than 300 crocodiles survive in the wild today.

AMERICAN CROCODILE

Crocodylus acutus

Historic Range: Florida, Mexico, South America, Central America, and the Caribbean.

Current Range: Small populations throughout historic range.

Estimated Wild Population: Approximately 200 to 300.

Estimated Captive Population: Undetermined numbers exist in zoos and circuses.

Major Threats: Human encroachment on habitats; poaching for skins and sport.

Conservation Efforts: Protection of habitats; enforcement of anti-poaching laws, captive breeding successful if release sites available and habitat protected.

KOMODO ISLAND MONITOR

If your idea of a lizard large enough to devour a person exists only in old television movies, think again. Such a lizard does exist, and has been known to lunch on humans. This appealing creature is the Komodo Island monitor, also called (and perhaps more appropriately) the Komodo dragon.

The dragon is not a typical lizard; a full-grown Komodo attains a length of ten feet (3 m) or more and weighs about 300 pounds (135 kg). They are thought to live at least 100 years.

In spite of their great size, they are swift runners, capable swimmers, and agile climbers.

The Komodo is a meat eater that feeds well on carrion, but is also capable of killing its own food—usually wild boar and deer. The lizard disables its prey with a vicious sideswipe of its tail.

The dragon once inhabited many of the islands of Indonesia but is now restricted to the islands of Komodo, Flores, Pintja, and Pada, east of Java. Its population has decreased steadily due to collecting, hunting for sport and to sell dragon hides, and from human encroachment into its habitat.

It may look like a monster from a science fiction movie, but the Komodo Island monitor is for real. Adult dragons may be more than 10 feet (3 m) long and weigh 300 pounds (135 kg).

KOMODO ISLAND MONITOR
Varanus komodensis

Historic Range: Islands of Indonesia.

Current Range: Small populations on islands east of Java.

Estimated Wild Population: Unknown.

Estimated Captive Population: In zoos.

Major Threats: Populations declined from overcollecting, dragon hunting.

Conservation Efforts: Protected under Endangered Species Act, which restricts collection and killing, and commercial trade bans discourage the selling of hides.

© Hank Klein/Ellis Wildlife Collection

The Galapagos giant tortoise prompted Charles Darwin to investigate the origin of species. Fossil records indicate that turtles were in existence some 200 million years ago.

GALAPAGOS TORTOISE

Before there were mammals, before there were birds, and before there were other reptiles, there were turtles. Fossil records indicate that turtles lumbered across the earth more than 200 million years ago. In some Native American cultures there is a story that the world is resting on the back of a turtle—hence one name for North America: Turtle Island.

Turtles are among the world's most long-lived species. French explorer Marion de Fresne collected five tortoises in 1776 and brought them to Mauritius. The British later occupied Mauritius and kept the five tortoises in captivity at the Royal barracks. The last of these five tortoises, captured in 1776, died in 1918. The tortoise was an adult when captured and its exact age was unknown. The animal could have been considerably older than the 142 years spent in captivity.

The turtle's shell makes the animal unique among the vertebrates and separates turtles from all others. The upper shell that covers the turtle's back is called the "carapace"; the lower shell is called the "plastron."

While all turtles have shells, each species has adapted differently to its environment, and there is much diversity among the more than 200 turtle species alive today. Some shells, especially in some strictly aquatic species, are more leathery in texture.

Tortoise shell has long been coveted by humans for its beautiful patterns and durability. Tortoises have been hunted for centuries for their shells, and many cultures consider turtle meat a delicacy.

Thousands of giant tortoises roamed the Galapagos Islands when explorers discovered them in the 1500s. With an average shell length of 5 feet (1.5 m) and weighing as much as 700 pounds (315 kg), the Galapagos giant tortoise is the most impressive of all terrestrial turtle species.

It's no wonder that explorers and whalers stopping at the Galapagos saw the giant tortoises as a valuable resource. Easily caught and killed, and just as easily kept alive on board ship for months or years at a time, the tortoises could provide a continuous supply of fresh meat. As early as the nineteenth century, the population of giant tortoises was dwindling.

To Charles Darwin, the Galapagos tortoise was a revelation. His observations of several subspecies of the Galapagos tortoise prompted his famous investigations into the origin of species. Today, at least three of the estimated 14 subspecies of the giant tortoise are extinct; the remaining species are endangered.

GALAPAGOS GIANT TORTOISE
Geochelone elephantopus

Historic Range: Galapagos Islands.

Current Range: Galapagos Islands.

Estimated Wild Population: Unknown.

Estimated Captive Population: A few have been successfully captive bred in zoos.

Major Threats: Human predation for meat during the nineteenth century substantially reduced numbers. Major threats today are predation of eggs and hatchlings by feral cats, pigs, dogs, and rats introduced to the Galapagos Islands. Habitat destruction by feral donkeys and goats is also a problem.

Conservation Efforts: Protection of habitat from excessive tourism, some control of introduced feral species. Captive breeding programs in zoos.

SEA TURTLES

All seven species of sea turtles are listed as endangered or threatened. These great turtles have been killed for their meat, skin, shells, and eggs. Although they are fairly safe in the open sea, a marine turtle on the beach becomes easy prey for human hunters, who know that the turtles favor particular beaches to lay their eggs, to which they return year after year. The turtle's egg-laying schedule is so predictable that, at the appropriate time, human predators have been known to wait on the beach to kill the turtles when they arrive.

Many turtles have died from ingesting plastic balloons and other debris dumped in the ocean; many more are victims of driftnets and ghost nets.

The green sea turtle swims the oceans but comes ashore to breed. Once on land, it is an easy victim of predators both human and animal.

GREEN SEA TURTLE

Chelonia mydas

Historic Range: Circumglobal in tropical and temperate seas.

Current Range: As above.

Estimated Wild Population: Unavailable.

Estimated Captive Population: Unavailable.

Major Threats: Hunting for use of meat, skin, shells. Most turtles are taken when they come ashore to lay eggs. Egg destruction by humans and predators; hatchling turtles are eaten by birds and other animals before reaching the safety of the water. Ghost nets; sludge and toxic wastes in ocean, especially plastics and similar materials, which the turtles mistake for food and ingest.

Conservation Efforts: The Sea Turtle is listed as a threatened species wherever it is found except at breeding sites in Florida and the Pacific Coast of Mexico, where it is endangered and receives protection under the ESA. Conservation groups monitor egg-laying to protect turtles from poachers.

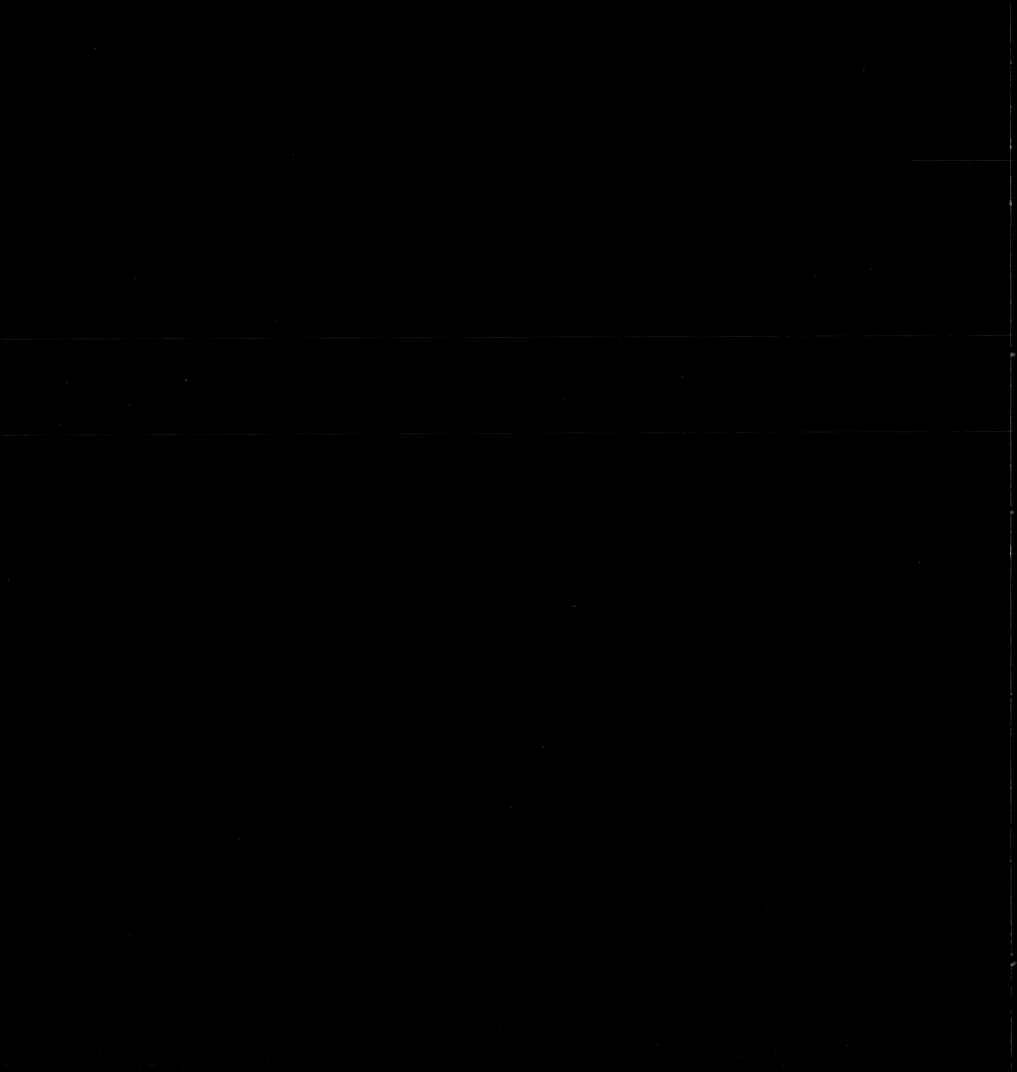

ENDANGERED FISH

Commercial fishermen in Japan, Norway, Portugal, and other countries have decimated blue fin tuna populations. Sport fishermen have also contributed to the slaughter, eliminating thousands of older, larger, reproducing tuna.

PELAGIC (SALTWATER) FISH

Considering the vastness of the world's oceans, it seems incomprehensible that these waters are not healthy enough to support the creatures that inhabit them. Yet the survival of the uncountable species that live in the earth's oceans is questionable. The oceans, after all, are limitless in their abundance—or are they?

In the most obvious example, humans have very nearly exhausted the ocean's supply of great whales. In a relatively short time, given the length of time that these majestic creatures swam the world's oceans unthreatened, humans have hunted the whales almost to extinction. Today, all of the great whales are listed as endangered species. Their plight has received worldwide attention through the efforts of the media and many conservation organizations, and now whales are finally receiving some measure of protection.

Fish have not been as fortunate, and little has been done to bring worldwide attention to their dwindling numbers. The culprits are mainly pollution and commercial fishing, and the commercial fisheries around the globe are well aware of diminishing supplies.

The methods used by commercial fisheries to catch large quantities of fish contribute to their declining populations. Longlines (line laid just below the surface that suspends hundreds of hooks) may stretch for 20 miles (32 km) or more, ruthlessly plundering the ocean's bounty. Yet it is the ubiquitous drift nets that probably have the most destructive impact. It was estimated that during the 1989 season, driftnet fishing was practiced by nearly 2,000 vessels in the North Pacific fisheries, collectively deploying approximately 30,000 miles (48,000 km) of net *every night*. Each net reaches from 25 to 50 feet (7.5 to 15 m) deep and may stretch across the ocean for 40 miles (64 km), trapping all the marine life in the area.

Although the nets are intended only for tuna, squid, and billfish, non-target species, including dolphins, porpoises, sharks, seals, turtles, seabirds, whales, and any other creatures that come into contact with the strong, nylon mesh, become entangled. Worse yet are the ghost nets—those that have broken loose and are "lost" at sea, endlessly capturing helpless creatures.

Although there have been few inquiries into the impact of driftnet fishing, some studies have revealed alarming statistics.

Off the coast of Alaska, during the 1986 salmon fishing season, a driftnet operation killed an estimated 14,000 Dall's porpoises and 750,000 seabirds in addition to its catch of fish. That same year, observers documented the deaths of 8 pilot whales, 2 killer whales, a large number of dolphins and porpoises, and 400 seabirds in a driftnet operation in Canadian waters.

It is feared that driftnet fishing, if continued unchecked, will threaten the very survival of the deepwater ocean ecosystem.

Pollution is equally dangerous to ocean life. Dumping of toxins and garbage, and ecosystem destruction due to such massive contamination as that caused by oil spills, wipes out vast numbers of fish each year. Yet ocean dumping continues unchecked, as seashores and ocean habitats wordwide are fouled and poisoned.

Fisheries in the Phillippine Islands catch tons of tropical fish by pumping cyanide into the coral reefs, which temporarily stuns the fish and makes for easy capture. This poison has also killed 95 percent of the reefs.

More than 99 million pounds (45 million kg) of plastics are dumped in our oceans annually. A single six-pack holder will survive in the water for 500 years—far longer than these endangered species and possibly, far longer than humanity itself. Many marine animals choke and strangle on our plastic waste, which they mistake for food or, in the case of plastic rings, which slip over their heads when they are small, and strangle them as they grow.

Much of this tragic destruction is hidden from human eyes, since it does not occur in front of us. Nevertheless, the problems are caused by our carelessness, and the solutions must also be our responsibility.

BLUEFIN TUNA
Thunnus thynnus thynnus

Though not yet listed as an endangered species, the bluefin and other species of tuna have suffered sharp declines due to overfishing. The Atlantic population is considered to be in a "depressed condition."

Historic Range: Widespread in the world's oceans.

Current Range: As above, in considerably lower numbers.

Estimated Wild Population: Unavailable.

Estimated Captive Population: Unavailable.

Major Threats: Overfishing. Estimated commercial world catch for 1981 was 1,815,000 tons (1,650,000 metric tons). Bluefin do not reproduce until they reach about 8 years of age; many are caught before spawning.

Conservation Efforts: Establishment of quotas, size limits, and other restrictions on fishing methods by various world governments, but fish population shows little sign of recovery.

FRESHWATER FISH

Fish are less visible to us than other creatures of the wild, because they live in water and are rarely seen. Yet they are no less significant in the natural order of things than any other creature. Indeed, we may already have lost many species of fish, with consequences that we do not yet understand. The list of endangered species of the world includes whole families of fishes, from the chubs to the darters, from pupfish and shiners to suckers and trout. Many of the fish on the list of endangered species are found in dry regions of the world, where water is scarce to begin with, and clean water even rarer.

In many desert regions, overgrazing has removed protective plants from riverbanks, allowing soil erosion to alter landscape and riverside, destroying fish habitats. Even without human interference, water in the desert is a scarce thing—and the desert fishes are among the most endangered species in the world. Some are found in a single specific location and nowhere else.

The locations of some of the surviving species are reflected in their names, especially among the pupfish: Devil's Hole pupfish, Leon Springs pupfish, Warm Springs pupfish, Comanche Springs pupfish. Of these, the Leon Springs pupfish has not been seen in over 100 years, and may be extinct. The Devil's Hole pupfish exists in a single, spring-fed pool in Nevada.

Lake and river fish are also endangered. Most river fish have declined in numbers due to the pollution of rivers, caused by river dumping, and by changes to the fragile landscape surrounding them. Damming rivers restricts the natural flow and cleansing of the waters and allows contamination levels to rise.

© Howard Burge/U.S. Fish and Wildlife Service

CUI-UI
(Chamistes cujus)

Historic Range: The Truckee River and Pyramid Lake in Nevada, Klamath Lake and tributaries in Oregon and California, and Utah Lake in Utah.

Current Range: Only in the Truckee River, Nevada.

Estimated Wild Population: In 1987, approximately 4,000 cui-ui were counted by biologists in the Truckee River.

Estimated Captive Population: Unknown.

Major Threats: Dams and water diversion projects on the cui-ui's native rivers have reduced water quality and drastically altered its habitat. Until 1987, the Truckee River Dam cut off the cui-ui's access to its spawning grounds, preventing the population from breeding.

Conservation Efforts: Habitat restoration: The U.S. Fish and Wildlife Service plans to restore a portion of the Truckee River and Pyramid Lake to its natural condition. A captive breeding program is underway to restock Pyramid Lake. The Marble Bluff Fish Facility was built to help the fish bypass the Truckee River Dam so they can reach their spawning grounds.

Even without dumping, pollution finds its way into lakes and rivers. Acid rain and industrial pollutants travel through the groundwater systems, poisoning bodies of water that cannot rid themselves of the toxins. All the life in the waters is affected.

Polluted rivers and lakes affect not only the fish species that live in them, but predators further up the food chain that feed on them. Concentrations of poison may be small enough in a single fish to allow its survival, but multiply the concentration of poison ingested by an eagle or bear or otter that consumes several fish a day, and those animals begin to experience the effects of the toxins. Mutations, disease, and sterility may result. The chemicals are passed on to humans who eat contaminated fish. At this time, for example, it is recommended that a person eat no more than 11 meals derived from Great Lakes fish in a lifetime. Pregnant women and children are advised to avoid them entirely.

In order to preserve the fish, we must learn to respect the lakes and rivers in which they live.

The construction of dams on their native rivers and degraded water quality have threatened the survival of the cui-ui. But if current plans to reclaim their natural habitat are successful, these fish stand a good chance of making a comeback.

© Howard Burge/U.S. Fish and Wildlife Service

Plugging the Holes

Through the pages of this book, you have become acquainted with a few of the animals the world is in danger of losing. There are literally thousands more that we have not mentioned, and more still whose survival status is yet unkown.

It is inevitable that certain species will die out and become extinct, no matter what we do. Perhaps they have reached the end of their evolutionary process. But most endangered animals today have that status because their evolutionary process has been disrupted, changed, and cut short by human interference. However, in altering the evolutionary process of these species, the human race is cutting short its own time.

In the past few years, a new human awareness of and respect for the environment has grown, out of concern that we are running out of time, because we are, literally, running out of planet.

Humans have been painfully slow learners in matters of the environment. A person's attitude can change quickly, however, once he or she realizes that each one of us is an important, yet fragile,

© Jeff Foott

MANATEE WATCH

thread in the overall tapestry. Suddenly, everything makes sense. People get perspective on the situation and change their wasteful life-styles. They recycle. They learn all they can about the environment, the earth, its animals, and the governments that make laws. They organize against those whose actions would further harm the earth. They work to repair damage that has already been done.

These people realize what will happen if the destruction is allowed to continue. They realize, too, that *all* of the threads in the tapestry must be tied, or the holes cannot be plugged.

Saving endangered species is an important part of repairing the tapestry. But unless we work to save the planet as well, *Homo sapiens* will inevitably join his brothers and sisters on the endangered species list.

At far left, an orphaned sea otter pup is cared for and fed. Left, conservationists attach a radio transmitter to a condor's wing in an attempt to monitor its flight. Above, the Crystal River in Florida supports a population of Florida manatees that is threatened by reckless boaters, but can coexist peacefully with more considerate humans.

APPENDICES

RESOURCES

Ready to grab a thread? There are hundreds of organizations that can provide guidance, education, materials, support, and encouragement to everyone interested in saving the earth. The following is a partial list of resources. It's a great way to start preserving *your* species on Earth. The first list provides addresses for associations linked to the specific animals in this book; the second is a general list of resources.

For more information on some of the endangered species in this book, contact the following organizations:

RABBIT BANDICOOT

Friends of the Earth
P.O. Box A474
Sydney South, NSW
Australia 2000

BROWN BEAR

Great Bear Foundation
P.O. Box 2699
Missoula, MT 59806

Wildlife Habitat Canada
1704 Carling Avenue, Suite 301
Ottawa, Ontario K2A 1C7

AFRICAN AND ASIAN ELEPHANTS

African Wildlife Foundation
1717 Massachusetts Avenue, N.W.
Washington, D.C. 20036

WWF India
B-1 Local Shopping Centre
J-Block, Saket
New Delhi, India 110017

MOUNTAIN GORILLA

Mountain Gorilla Project
African Wildlife Foundation
International Primate Protection
    League
P.O. Box 766
Summerville, SC 29484

SNOW LEOPARD

International Snow Leopard Trust
16463 Southeast 35th Street
Bellevue, WA 98008

FLORIDA MANATEE

Sea World of Florida
7007 Sea World Drive
Orlando, FL 32821

GIANT PANDA

WWF Panda Project
1250 24th Street, N.W.
Washington, D.C. 20037

Wildlife Conservation International
New York Zoological Society
Bronx, NY 10460

BLACK RHINOCEROS

American Association of Zoological
    Parks and Aquariums
4550 Montgomery Avenue,
    Suite 940N
Bethesda, MD 20814

THREE-TOED SLOTH

World Wildlife Fund International
Avenue du Mont Blanc
1196 Gland, Switzerland

WOLVES

Wild Canid Survival and Research
    Center
Wolf Sanctuary
P.O. Box 760
Eureka, MO 63025

EarthFirst! Wolf Action Network
P.O. Box 67333
Bozeman, MT 59771

VAQUITA

American Cetacean Society
P.O. Box 2639
San Pedro, CA 90731

RIGHT WHALE

Greenpeace U.S.A.
1436 U Street, N.W.
Washington, D.C. 20009

The Whale Center
3929 Piedmont Avenue
Oakland, CA 94611

SEA OTTER

Friends of the Sea Otter
P.O. Box 221220
Carmel, CA 93922

HONEYCREEPER

International Council for Bird
    Preservation
801 Pennsylvania Avenue, S.E.
Washington, D.C. 20003

FISH

Greenpeace Australia
Studio 14, 37 Nicholson St.
Balmain, NSW
2041 Australia

National Coalition for Marine
    Conservation
P.O. Box 23298
Savannah, GA 31403

North American Native Fishes
    Association
123 West Mt. Airy Avenue
Philadelphia, PA 19119

SPECIES SURVIVAL PLAN

The American Association of Zoological Parks and Aquariums (AAZPA) has initiated a program called the Species Survival Plan (SSP), as an intended "supplement, not an alternative, to preservation in nature."

Through the SSP, zoos, aquariums, and wildlife parks participate in captive-breeding programs for endangered species. According to the AAZPA, about one-sixth of all types of mammals and one-twelfth of the world's bird species have been bred successfully in zoos in the past few years.

Zoos involved in the SSP cooperate in matching unmated animals to enhance breeding results, and explore options such as embryo transfer and artificial insemination.

Elands (large African antelopes) have been successfully bred using embryo transfers, and healthy gaurs (East Indian wild oxen) have been born to Holstein cows after transfer of embryos.

Many endangered species are being successfully bred through this program. For more information contact:

The American Association of
Zoological Parks and Aquariums
Ogelbay Park
Wheeling, WV 26003

Some of the zoos participating in the SSP program, where many endangered species may be seen, are:

Birmingham Zoo,
Birmingham, AL

Phoenix Zoo,
Phoenix, AZ

San Diego Wild Animal Park,
Escondido, CA

San Diego Zoo,
San Diego, CA

Los Angeles Zoo,
Los Angeles, CA

Sacramento Zoo,
Sacramento, CA

Denver Zoological Gardens,
Denver, CO

Beardsley Zoo,
Bridgeport, CT

Miami Metro Zoo,
Miami, FL

Brookfield Zoo/Chicago Zoological
Park,
Brookfield, IL

Lincoln Park Zoo,
Chicago, IL

Blank Park Zoo,
Des Moines, IA

Detroit Zoological Park,
Royal Oak, MI

Minnesota Zoo,
Apple Valley, MN

St. Louis Zoological Park,
St. Louis, MO

Henry Doorly Zoo,
Omaha, NE

Rio Grande Zoological Park,
Albuquerque, NM

Bronx Zoo,
Bronx, NY

Seneca Park Zoo,
Rochester, NY

Staten Island Zoo,
Staten Island, NY

North Carolina Zoological Park,
Asheboro, NC

Oklahoma City Zoo,
Oklahoma City, OK

Roger Williams Park Zoo,
Providence, RI

Dallas Zoo,
Dallas, TX

Point Defiance Zoo and Aquarium,
Tacoma, WA

Milwaukee County Zoo,
Milwaukee, WI

For general information on endangered species, and to find out what you can do to help save the earth, contact the following organizations:

USA

Alliance for Environmental
Education
Box 1040, 3421 M Street, N.W.
Washington, D.C. 20007

Clean Water Action
733 15th Street, N.W.
Washington, D.C. 20005

The Cousteau Society
930 W. 21st Street
Norfolk, VA 23517

EarthFirst!
P.O. Box 2358
Lewiston, ME 04241

Earthscan
1717 Massachusetts Avenue, N.W.
Washington, D.C. 20036

Environmental Defense Fund
257 Park Avenue South
New York, NY 10010

Greenpeace, U.S.A.
1436 U Street, N.W.
Washington, D.C. 20009

International Oceanographic
Foundation
3979 Rickenbacker Causeway
Virginia Key
Miami, FL 33149

National Audubon Society
950 Third Avenue
New York, NY 10022

National Wildlife Federation
1412 16th Street, N.W.
Washington, D.C. 20036

The Nature Conservancy
1815 N. Lynn Street
Arlington, VA 22209

Rainforest Action Network
301 Broadway
San Francisco, CA 94133

Sierra Club
730 Polk Street
San Francisco, CA 94109

World Resources Institute
1709 New York Avenue, N.W.,
7th Floor
Washington, D.C. 20006

CANADA

WWF Canada
60 St. Clair Ave. E.
Suite 201
Toronto, Ontario M4T 1M5

Greenpeace Canada
2623 West 4th Ave.
Vancouver, BC V6K 1P8

Pollution Probe
12 Madison Ave.
Toronto, Canada MR5 2S1

Canadian Nature Federation
453 Sussex Drive
Ottawa, Ontario K1N 6Z4

Canadian Parks and Wilderness
 Society
69 Sherbourne Street, Suite 313
Toronto, Ontario M5A 3X7

Canadian Wildlife Federation
1673 Carling Avenue
Ottawa, Ontario K2A 3Z1

AUSTRALIA AND NEW ZEALAND

Greenpeace Australia
155 Pirie St.
Adelaide 5000

WWF Australia
Level L-7 St. Martins Tower
31 Market St.
Sydney, NSW 2001

Rainforest Action Group
P.O. Box 368
Lismore, NSW 2480

Australian Conservation Foundation
340 Gore St.
Fitzroy, Victoria 3065

The Wilderness Society
130 Davey St.
Hobart, TAS 7000

Greenpeace New Zealand
Private Bag, Wellesley St.
Auckland, NZ

UK

Greenpeace UK
30-31 Islington Green
London N1 8XE

Greenpeace Ireland
44 Upper Mount St.
Dublin 2, Eire

WWF-Panda House
Weyside Park
Godalming, Surrey BU7 1XE

Friends of the Earth
26-28 Underwood St.
London N1 75Q

Advisory Committee on Pollution of
 the Sea
3 Endsleigh St.
London WC1H 0DD

FURTHER READING

The following books are highly recommended:

Bergman, Charles. *Wild Echoes.* New York: McGraw Hill, 1990.

Caduto, Michael, and Joseph Bruchac. *Keepers of the Earth.* New York: Golden, Co., Fulcrum Inc., 1988.

Diamond, Schreiber, Cronkite, Peterson. *Save the Birds.* Boston: Houghton Mifflin, 1989.

Dominico, Terry. *Bears of the World.* New York: Facts on File, 1988.

Fossey, Dian. *Gorillas in the Mist.* Boston: Houghton Mifflin, 1983.

Hillard, Darla. *Vanishing Tracks: Four Years Among the Snow Leopards of Nepal.* New York: Arbor House/William Morrow, 1989.

Lopez, Barry. *Of Wolves and Men.* New York: Charles Scribner's & Sons, 1978.

Mech, L. David. *The Arctic Wolf.* Stillwater, Minn.: Voyageur Press, 1988.

Moss, Cynthia. *Elephant Memories.* New York: Ballantine, Del Rey, Fawcett, 1988.

Schaller, George, and Hu Jinshu, Pen Wenshi, Zu Jing. *The Giant Pandas of Wolong.* Chicago: University of Chicago Press, 1985.

INDEX